WHAT OTHERS ARE SAYING ABOUT *NURTURING CUSTOMER RELATIONSHIPS...*

"Jim Cecil and Nurture Marketing changed my life. Nurture is now ingrained into all that I do. The rewards from applying these basic life principles have been astounding. The business success from using nurturing is second only to the personal rewards I have received by virtue of utilizing these basic life principles. Jim Cecil is AWESOME!" —Andy Vabulas, President, IBIS, INC, Atlanta, GA

"After 24 years of training financial service professionals, I have to say this is the one book I can recommend without hesitation. There's no fluff – just an easy to understand series of stories, examples and actual steps for creating your own ethical customer relationship process. Jim Cecil is the best marketing mind I've ever met. Incredibly, this book absolutely captures the essence of his vast experience and insights. I've ordered a case for my clients and colleagues." —Bud Elsea, President, Bud Elsea Productions, Norcross, GA

"Great book with a lot of solid ideas to grow your business and customer relationships. Putting Jim's sound business practices into place will not only assist you in reaching your sales goals, it will also put your company ahead of your competition in service and customer relationships." —Walt Gdowski, Publisher, Rough Notes Magazine, Carmel, IN

Nurturing Customer Rel

D1399874

"I first learned nurture marketing from Jim Cecil. It has completely changed my business and our clients' businesses. If you want an easy, stress-free way of finding client advocates, let Jim show you the way" — Katherine Vessenes, JD, CFP(R), President, Vestment Advisors, Minneapolis, MN

"Few people understand the philosophy, the technology and the methodology of cultivating relationships with top level executives in global class organizations as well as Jim Cecil. I have implemented Nurture in my own company with results that have made me a true believer. I loved this book. It is cleanly written, and includes the actual ethical steps and strategies necessary to implement a high touch relationship process and to gain and retain top-of-mind with important prospects and clients. A must read for those selling at the top of the food chain." —Randy Casey, Founder and Managing Partner, Ashland Group L.P., Houston, TX

"This book truly is a transformational business tool for use in today's highly competitive global marketplace. It is a 'must read' for those who want to increase endorsements with their clients and employees. Seven years ago, my staff and I attended one of Jim's Nurture Marketing training workshops. Since then, my business has more than doubled and has grown both nationally and internationally. His nurture marketing principles are right on target! Thanks, Jim, for your support over the years and for teaching me how to nurture my clients." — Judy Suiter, President, Competitive Edge, Inc., Peachtree City, GA

"*In a world crying out for care,* Nurturing Customer Relationships *comes along at the perfect time. From its compelling philosophical grounding to practical applications, it is profound in its elegance and simplicity.* Nurturing Customer Relationships *brings it all together. Throw commoditization out the window. This is a 'can't miss' opportunity for companies to take their marketing and sales effort to the next level. 'Nurturing' works. As Jim Cecil so wisely invites... Test it!"* —Jim Kelly, Lt Col, USAF, Ret, and President and Co-Founder of Kelly-Stanton Group, Novato, CA

If nurture marketing has a guru, it has to be Jim Cecil. We try to tell his 'drip irrigation' story to all our insurance agency members. After hearing Jim speak and reading this book and many of his 'nurture' writings, we set up a division of our business to use the principles we learned from him. This book should be required reading for everyone wanting to know the number one marketing theorem: "Nurture Your Clients". —George Nordhaus, Chairman, IMMS, Los Angeles, CA

.

Nurturing Customer Relationships

JIM CECIL & ERIC RABINOWITZ

With Carol Ellison and Karin Rex

First Edition

Nurture Institute Press

To Tony Cecil,
my dad, my mentor and my hero.
— Jim Cecil

To my wife Cindy, my daughter Jodi and son
David whose love and support have nurtured me
throughout my life. To Jeff Leska, the brother I never
had. And to Jim Cecil, a truly great man who has shared
his passion for which I am eternally grateful.
— Eric S. Rabinowitz

TABLE OF CONTENTS

Foreword

Nurture is a remarkable word. It is certainly a word a person would have trouble saying in anger. The word has a peaceful softness to it, as it should since it stems from the Babylonian word "nutra" which means to breast feed or nourish. But whether you are referring to raising a child or growing a business, nurturing involves more than just basic care. It requires intensive all-encompassing care. It is more than just feeling love or saying, "I love you,"—it means actively showing it.

I have adopted Nurture as the perfect metaphor for my personal and professional life. It is the fundamental tenet behind the concept of Nurture Marketing that I have been preaching for years. It is the principle behind the Nurture Selling Process that my co-author and fellow nurturer, Eric Rabinowitz, and I present in this book.

Eric is a person I have nurtured since we met in 1992 and who, in turn, has nurtured. Back then, he was one of my best and most loyal clients. Today, he leads our course development at the Nurture Institute. As Chief Executive Officer of DEMA Education, an organization dedicated to developing targeted training programs for companies in emerging markets, Eric is committed to showing clients how to increase their companies' strategic value to their customers and add new revenue sources to their business through training.

The Nurture Selling Process, which we present here, is our "cure for the common cold call." It is a systematic approach to nurturing clients and customers, one that leverages technology to build and maintain customer loyalty.

Karin Rex, a writer with a long and admirable record in training courseware development and writing, joins us in bringing you this book. Karin is the founder of ComputerEase, a company that specializes in customized training and eLearning. She adds her expertise as the author of several technology and business books, and hundreds of guides, reference manuals, tutorials, course manuals, and articles.

We also wish to thank Carol Ellison, an award-winning journalist whose in-depth case studies and diligent editing made this book possible. I have known Carol since her days as a senior and executive editor with one of the nation's largest publishers. Today she is principal owner of Ellison Associates, a custom authoring house that specializes in "Stories That Sell."

That is our team. The rest of this book talks about yours. It is all about how a properly nurtured team, one that in turn is willing to relentlessly nurture customers, can determine your long-term marketing success.

Jim Cecil
Bellevue, Washington

Chapter I—The Nature of Nurturing

"When you need a friend, it's too late to make one."

Mark Twain

CONTENTS

LESSONS FROM A FARMER

Even before I learned to ride a bicycle I learned what it took to win customers for life. That's the truth.

I learned that lesson at my father's knee when I was growing up as a boy in rural Kentucky during and after World War II. It wasn't a lesson about selling. It was a lesson about nurturing. It was a lesson about what it means to care about people and to let them know it and to prosper from their goodwill.

My father, Tony Cecil, sold farm equipment and he was good at it. He knew a sale could be quick and straight-forward. It could be as simple as helping a customer make a single purchase. But he also knew it could be time-consuming. It could be about not making a sale at all—at least not an immediate sale. He knew the sale might not happen today. It might not happen tomorrow. It might not happen even in a month or so. It could take a whole year or even two years.

But my father knew that if he stuck with those customers and helped them succeed at growing their businesses even when there wasn't an immediate sale in it for him, the customers would, in all probability, come back to my father when they were prepared to buy. Why? Because all of his help and hard work had earned him top-of-mind presence. And that's what this book is about—earning top-of-mind presence with your customers so that they come to you when they are ready to buy.

Dad understood that the energy he invested in the challenging and time-consuming process of helping farmers succeed would lead to long-lasting relationships.

My father was a perpetual student of small farms and an unabashed admirer of their owners. He studied nature intently and poured over the meager small-farm management knowledge available at the time in farm journals and books. He learned what successful farmers did to ensure their success and he ascertained what not-so-successful farmers did to undermine theirs. He became an expert at ferreting out solutions and made it his business to talk to the people who could provide those solutions. He listened eagerly to any and all tips from farm equipment factory representatives and he shared his knowledge with his customers.

He urged his customers to improve their processes and he urged them to measure those improvements. He won their lifelong loyalty by pointing them to new ideas and solutions. He made successful customers more successful and helped the less-than-successful turn their fortunes around.

Dad stayed in touch with his customers through postcards. And he didn't just pitch a used equipment deal or a tractor sale on those postcards. He gave them something of value – a seasonal tip, perhaps, or a unique horticultural insight. And he never failed to conclude his notes with a wish for the farmer's successful harvest. He believed in the Biblical truth, "As you sow, so shall you reap," and he put that belief into action.

This book is about applying that belief to business. It is about achieving a top-of-mind presence with our customers. It is about taking a serious approach to attracting and retaining and growing your customer relationships to build a continuum of prosperity for your business. It is about the vision we must bring to marketing efforts to succeed in the 21st century. And it is about measurement and the tools we need to put that vision to work.

Tools are an important part of this equation. I once heard Bill Gates, co-founder of Microsoft, tell an audience, "We can no more appreciate the impact of today's technologies on the future than the person who invented the first stone knife could imagine the carvings on the doors of Sistine Chapel."

Success in business means knowing how to apply the tools at your disposal in just the right way to carve customer relationships that are elegant and timeless.

You will read about all of this in later chapters. But, here in Chapter 1, I want to talk about nurturing and how, over the years, I realized that the lessons I learned down on the farm are the perfect metaphor for business success.

WHAT NURTURING IS

One of my chores as a young boy was to water the family garden. I used to carry water in a heavy metal bucket and dip it out with a hollow gourd to distribute it over the plants. That was my introduction to the notion of drip irrigation. It wasn't easy work but my father showed me that my continual, attentive care of those plants was directly responsible for a successful harvest. Without it there would be no bumper crop.

Nurturing coincides perfectly with the theory of customer-touching. The parallels between successfully cultivating a farm and successfully marketing a business are many. When I consider the art of sales and marketing and what it means to win customer loyalty—loyalty that you retain over the life of your relationship with that customer—I often reflect upon the examples gently planted by my father in my earliest memories.

In farming and in marketing we seek bountiful harvests. That requires patience and an investment in time. That's not always easy in the fast times we live in today. But clients, like crops, must be fed, nourished, protected, cultivated, pruned, and pampered to ensure maximum results.

There is a direct correlation between the kind of drip irrigation I practiced with my gourd on the Kentucky farm where I grew up and the drip-marketing theories we're reading about in business literature today.

Nurture may be a metaphor but it is also a philosophy. It deals with people as human beings and shows us the value of treating others as we would want to be treated.

The farmer knows that the result of the harvest is always the result of the care and skill he or she devotes to the task of cultivation. In business it is not a bad metaphor to think of yourself as a farmer even if you've never had dirt on your hands—primarily because, as I said earlier, all living things respond to nurturing.

Nurturers truly care about people and are passionate about what they do. They take a long-term view of growing their businesses and their employees, clients, and vendor relationships. For the nurturer, creating experiences around those relationships is a life-long endeavor. Nurturers are givers more than takers. Ethics are important in their lives and their businesses.

I love the metaphor of human beings as plants in our garden. Our success is dependent on our skill in nurturing them.

Nurture marketing is the name we give to the marketing strategy that nurtures customer relationships. In these times of dynamic change where the forces that impact business can change in the course of a day, Nurture Marketing provides a steady key to success in the business-to-business sales process.

Nurture marketing is about making your sales team more productive and focused on earning lifelong customer loyalties. It is not about changing people. I do not know how to do that. I do not think anybody does. Instead it is about influence and how you gain it by touching hearts and minds.

In sales we are exposed to all the incentives of motivation early in our working careers. Salespeople have seen the carrots dangled before them—raises, bonuses, big cars, and all-expense-paid vacations.

When they do not produce it is not because they lack motivation. What is lacking is stimulation to act on those motivations. That is management's job—to stimulate our pursuit of success. And, as executives, that is where we get into trouble. The problem is, we do not know what motivates them. Nurture Marketing has as much to do with caring for our internal staff, particularly our sales teams, as it does with caring for our clients. It is about caring for—and motivating—every person in the organization whose job touches customers so that they, in turn, will nurture customers and show them that your company is one that will be there for them.

WHAT NURTURING IS NOT

Nurture marketing is not what many other contemporary sales techniques are all about. It does not get in the client's face with communications designed to deceive, distract, fool, or seduce them into buying. Nurture marketing respects clients as intelligent and thoughtful human beings. And for that reason, in these days of spam and in-your-face advertising, it has great appeal among customers. Nurturing connects people at a spiritual level because it is gentle, honest, helpful, and truthful. It crosses the boundaries that separate people and promises relationships grounded in good faith.

Nurture marketing does not replace sales. It accelerates and leverages your sales efforts. Nurturing is about proactively pampering and assisting an individual through all the phases of a buying and owning process. Nurture marketing enhances every segment of a customer-relationship-driven organization giving dimension and purpose to the concept of customer intimacy and affection.

Nurturing is not a quick fix for sagging sales figures. It is not about eliciting a response from every contact. It is about attaining and retaining a top-of-mind position with your client or prospect. It is a long-term commitment to helping clients succeed.

Don't confuse nurture marketing with direct mail. Most direct mail solicitations—whether they are invitations, offers, announcements, or sales appeals—demand that the client responds by a specified time. *"Reply within 10 days for a special discount!"* Most clients want their "special discount" when they are ready to buy, not just when you are ready to sell. Nurture marketing, unlike direct mail, is not time-dependent. Instead, it aligns with the client's actual buying process. Such flexibility provides the freedom to initiate and sustain a relationship at any point in a client's buying cycle and is attentive to changes in the relationship.

Nurturing is not advertising. David Ogilvy, founder of Ogilvy & Mather, said "mass advertising is essentially climbing the tallest hill, using the loudest voice and reaching the maximum number of ears with the same message as many times as you can afford." Not only are mass selling techniques such as advertising expensive, they work only if most of the people seeing your advertisement need exactly what you're offering at exactly the time your advertisement appears.

Nurture marketing is not magic. It is a powerful, automatable process that can be defined, documented, and repeated. The purpose of this book is to introduce you to that process. The goal of nurturing contacts, whether through letters or calls, is not to coerce a client to take action now. It is to cultivate a positive top-of-mind awareness for your services or product with that client.

HARVESTS OF FAITH

A few years back I happened upon an amazing example of the power of nurturing during a visit to JiuZhaiGuo in the western Chinese Province of Chengdu. I had been invited to speak at a marketing conference and, having spent my boyhood on a farm, I wanted to see the countryside while I was there. One of the local officials introduced me to his brother-in law, 75-year-old Ping-Sun (Peter) Liu, who had an oxcart with a bench just big enough to haul me around. Peter spoke enough English that we could communicate and we spent an amazing day together.

He took me to a construction site that was being built for tourism, to a factory to show me how rapidly the country was moving from a feudal economy into modern times, and to his home to have lunch with his family. But I specifically wanted to see farms, so after lunch he took me down this long road and that is where I learned about "black bamboo" and persistence.

Bamboo, as you know, is a grass and there are thousands of varieties of it. Black bamboo is the one with the highest tensile strength, is the tallest and one of the strongest natural substances in the world. It is so strong that it supports the scaffolding for construction that is making the Pacific Rim the economic wonder it is today. If you have been to Hong Kong or any of the major Chinese cities, you have seen black bamboo poles lashed together in scaffolding that brackets skyscrapers as high as 60 stories.

Black bamboo is the perfect peasant crop in China's emerging free enterprise economy. The seeds are given free to farmers simply for agreeing to grow it. There is high demand for it due to the profitable pace of economic growth.

Not surprisingly black bamboo is one of the most popular crops in China. The first field we visited looked like an empty field of tilled earth. Peter explained that when the field had been sowed a few weeks earlier more than a thousand farmers each carried a satchel of seeds with water and fertilizer into the field. The farmers planted only the seeds that had the best chance for success, and they perfectly positioned them in the ground—not too deep and not too shallow—to prevent birds and other animals (their competitors) from beating them to the harvest. This also prevented each seed from competing with each other for food and water, allowing each plant to grow to its full potential.

Our next stop was a field that had been sowed two years prior. There we saw thousands of farmers working in what looked like an empty field. They went back and forth, feeding muddy mounds where the individual seeds were planted—imagine all that effort with no promise of results until the seeds started to sprout and they could see the results of their hard work.

They watered and fed each seed every week, never missing a week. The farmers did this without modern irrigation or fertilizer. Their answer to fertilizer was a slurry they created by hauling dung into a pond. They'd dip up that slurry and carry it to the fields in bags over their shoulders. Then, over each seed, they would squeeze the bag and release a quart of slurry.

In the 59th month, after almost five full years of hard work, all of a sudden, the seedlings would suddenly shoot up out of the ground and grow to 60 feet in 30 days! It is probably the fastest growing crop in the world once it comes out of the ground. You can literally watch it grow in front of your eyes. The difficulty, obviously, was that the farmer never really knew if he had a crop until the shoots started soaring out of the ground. That's why Peter called it a "crop of faith."

Modern business can learn a lesson from that feudal economy because the black bamboo seed is basically a nut with a very tough skin. Does that describe some of your customers? Nuts that are tough to crack? Tough customers must be pampered before "the sprout" of a relationship can penetrate their tough skin. I once had a CEO tell me, "You'd better not be here to pluck me like an apple. You have to pamper me like an orchid."

How many of your customers do you pamper like an orchid? If you were a farmer would you give up on a crop like black bamboo? Sometimes the toughest crops to grow, the ones like orchids and black bamboo, are the ones that return the greatest rewards. Short-term thinkers in business will not be around to reap those rewards. They don't realize that customer relationships are a lot like black bamboo.

The question to ask here is: "When did all that growth really take place?" Did the plant grow 60 feet in one month or in five years? The answer is obvious—growth was a result of consistent cultivation throughout all five years! Had the farmer neglected those plants at any time during those five years, the harvest would not have happened.

Nurturing is like that.

You may cultivate a client faithfully for years with seemingly no results and then all of a sudden they are ready to buy and they call you. They call you because you've been there all along, nurturing them. They call you because they think of you first.

But there's more to this story about the black bamboo. We visited one more field and there we saw many long bamboo poles lying flat in the mud as far as the eye could see. If you recall the photographs of the flattened forests after Mt. St. Helens erupted in 1980 you have some idea of how it looked. I wondered what happened to that field so, pointing toward it, I asked Peter, "Typhoon?" He had a curious answer. "Fool farmer", he replied. It seems that farmer had not nurtured his crop properly. The crop was weak and the wind had blown it over. "Fool farmer," he repeated. And then he shook his head and said, "Five years wasted."

I like to tell that black bamboo story because it demonstrates how the farming metaphor applies to nurture marketing at every level. Nurture marketing is about caring for your clients in your heart of hearts and letting them know it through the kind of attentive, persistent care the black bamboo farmer gives his crop. It is about continuing that care all the way to harvest and knowing that the products and services you deliver are the perfect fit for your clients' needs.

Long-term customer relationships are "harvests of faith." We engage in those relationships for mutual benefit. We expect our customers will benefit from what we have to sell and we have faith they will come to us when they need what we have to sell. We have to trust that our reward for all the care we invest in that relationship will come with time. We have to be willing to spend the time and the resources to invest in those relationships with no firm promise of future returns. We may not reap the result of our care for many years, but if we do not make the investment, there will be no customer relationship.

If you are not doing all you can to care for that customer relationship, you are out of sight of that customer, and if you are out of sight of the customer, chances are, all you are doing is "cold-calling". Know what I say about cold calls? They get chilly receptions. Mae West said it like this: "Out of sight is out of mind, and out of mind is out of money, honey."

THE STRATEGY OF NURTURING

Peter Drucker said that the difference between marketing and sales is that marketing is about strategy and sales are about tactics. Nurturing is about strategy—a strategy that helps others grow, and those we help grow will, in turn, contribute to our growth.

In businesses today there is much talk about strategies, especially strategies for success. My father certainly applied a nurturing strategy to his business, but, back then, he would have told you it was just a matter of helping customers in the same way one helps a friend.

I like to use farm metaphors to describe sales—sales are the harvest, or what we reap; marketing is the planning and nurturing strategy we use to ensure the abundant harvest.

Someone must do the nurturing. Someone must do the planting. Someone must do some side-dressing and some pruning and pinching in order for human beings to grow into a relationship where they trust us enough to enter into an alliance.

The soil for meaningful alliances is more fertile now than it has ever been. Downsizing has created a new dynamic. Today, business customers are in the market for specialists. They need your expertise. They need your intelligence. They need your wisdom and they need your contacts. Not so long ago companies were able to evaluate products they needed, and once purchased, install the equipment themselves. They could literally go out to bid, match your offering on price, and handle their own deployments. Today, customers are looking for much more—they need your help in solving their business problems. They need reassurance that you are the one who can deliver the care they need when they need it.

Nurturing is a process that devotes systematic attention to the customer—the same sort of persistent attention the Chinese farmers devote to the black bamboo.

The nurturing process is a powerful marketing strategy fueled by fresh new technology and is an innovative and highly personal method of communicating with clients and prospects.

The process is designed to give you "top of mind" position with your clients, making them far more likely to call you the moment they are ready to buy.

Additionally, the nurturing process helps you to be more efficient and effective, and builds a long-lasting relationship that keeps them coming back to you.

Nurturing also provides the power to reactivate and leverage lost or non-productive relationships.

Once you have gained top-of-mind awareness, nurturing continues to reinforce the message you are sending. It defends your top-of-mind position against competitive attacks and provides a systematic approach for proactively demonstrating your unique business style. It also enables you to manage your relationships with awareness, trust, respect, and precision.

But it takes persistence. Short-term thinkers focus on short-term results. If an initiative does not produce immediate results, it is often abandoned too quickly. Long-term thinkers who are in it for the long haul realize that persistence and patience will eventually pay off.

The best producers do not give up. They send letters, make time to visit their clients, make telephone calls, and continue making new contacts within the company. They persist in following up until a prospect either a) chooses a competitor; b) is no longer in the market (having literally or figuratively died); or c) until the client is theirs. Persistence with CARE (Consistent, Appropriate, Respectful, and Effective) promotes awareness and differentiation, and encourages a client's interest to grow naturally.

Nurturing is about communicating the right message to the right people at the right time.

It always works. You just need to do it.

Chapter II—The Power of Staying in Touch

"Customers, when given a choice of where they spend their money, invariably go back to that place where they have consistently and intentionally been made to feel special."

Marshall Field

CONTENTS

EMOTIONAL BANK ACCOUNTS

After the great Chicago fire of 1917, Marshall Field looked down on the crumbled ashes of his store. Everyone else was leaving town, but he announced he would rebuild. Why? Because he knew his customers would come back. When given a choice, Field said, customers invariably go back to a place where they have been made to feel special.

Businesses don't buy anything. People buy. Marshall Field knew that.

Human beings, just like those plants I watered in my family garden as a boy, thrive on pampering. Pampering is probably the most addictive substance in the universe. It is irresistible. When we frequent a particular restaurant, the owner recognizes us and makes a fuss—"Jim's here. Quick, clean up the table by the window. Get his favorite wine." We experience such pampering and, predictably, feel welcomed and reassured that our patronage is appreciated.

Have you noticed how that kind of pampering builds loyalty? We will go back to that restaurant again and again. Why? Because we know we will be made to feel special there. We perceive the owner to be an attentive person, not someone who is simply out to take our money but someone who takes care of us, who has earned our patronage and made deposits in our "emotional bank account."

In his book, *The Seven Habits of Highly Effective People,* Stephen Covey uses the metaphor of the "emotional bank account" as a measure of the trust that has been built up in a relationship. To create truly important relationships you must make deposits into that account before asking for anything in return.

Each time you, as a business person, do something that your client perceives as a kind, caring or serving act (which is really what nurturing is all about), you are making a deposit into the shared emotional bank account you have with that client.

Deposits are not self-serving. They are actions that truly serve the recipient. They are a demonstration of respect, kindness, courtesy, and your appreciation of their business. Appropriate gifts, given sincerely and with no strings attached, are deposits. An item as small as an article of relevance to the individual, torn from a newspaper or magazine, is often a tangible demonstration of the value you feel toward that customer. Since your gift or act of kindness is about "the customer" and their hopes or fears, and not about you, it is perceived as a deposit into an important and growing relationship.

Withdrawals are exactly the opposite. Each time you behave in a manner that your client perceives as self-serving, you are making a withdrawal from that shared emotional bank account.

A face-to-face meeting which might be welcomed by one client might also be perceived as a negative step in the eyes of another client if it occurs prematurely, before the client relationship has matured. Asking a client for a favor—an introduction or referral to another potential prospect is a serious withdrawal unless you have earned the right to ask for it. So is asking for the sale too early.

THE RELENTLESS PURSUIT OF LOW-HANGING FRUIT

A cold call is a withdrawal. When you make a cold call you are asking for a withdrawal (their time) from the customer relationship before you have made any deposits.

If all you are doing is cold calling, you may be seriously overdrawing the emotional bank accounts you share with the people whose business you want. When an emotional bank account is overdrawn, that relationship is in jeopardy.

If you agree with Marshall Field that when people have choices regarding where they spend their money, they invariably go back to a place where they have been made to feel special, you also accept the premise that making a sale on a cold call is pure luck.

It is amazing that cold calling is still such a popular method for trying to find new clients. The successful cold call really is the "luck of the draw". A cold call requires that you speak to the right person at the precise time that person has a need for what you are selling, and whose budget can accommodate your specific product or service. If all those stars are not in alignment, there is no sale.

It is certainly disheartening to learn that a customer has made their purchase only a month before meeting with you, isn't it?

Bumper crops are the result of very specific strategies and excellent execution. I have never met a farmer yet who went out into a field, threw seeds at random and said, "C'mon God, let's have a good rain year and I'll see you in the fall."

For the most part, any sale made on a cold call is likely a case of low-hanging fruit—someone who just happened to be ready to buy when you just happened to call.

Some companies report that they lose first-time customers twice as fast as established customers. Have you ever wondered why?

Could it be that these companies are spending more time courting customers than nurturing existing ones? Too many people still cling to the idea that, "If you build it, customers will come" and, "If you do good work, you will get referrals." That is nothing more than running a passive operation. One person called it the "prayer method" of marketing. It might have worked in the past but it is not working now. Today's business must be proactively pursued; messages must communicate, and it must all be done by design—not by accident.

Too many companies put the bulk of their marketing resources into attracting new customers. They bet the farm on one-shot offerings and, too often, what they get are one-time bargain hunters who are interested only in finding the lowest price.

The most important factor in a buying decision is often thought to be "price." But have you considered price in the context of customer loyalty? Most businesses try to attract new customers using introductory offers, but all the while the newcomers harvest your introductory offer, they are peering over the fence in search of greener pastures. Two questions should be asked: Are first-timers the customers you want? If so, what can you do to keep them?

In their book, *Return on Customer*, Don Peppers and Dr. Martha Rogers report that 6 out of 10 prospects will turn you down four times before they make a purchase. They maintain that the customers who are the easiest to get are the hardest to keep and those who are the toughest are most likely to become your best long-term customers.

Nurture marketing brings the simple, wholesome lessons of the farmer into the business world. It is all about cultivating life-long client relationships just as you nurture all the other relationships you value in life—your family, your friends, your job, your church or synagogue, your community, your pets—and, yes, your houseplants. Consider all the relationships that would wither without your attention. Customer relationships are no different. If you want the customer to think of you when he or she is ready to spend money, you must continue to touch that customer in spite of the fact that he or she might not be ready to buy at that moment. Customers operate on their own buying cycles. Success comes by ensuring that you will be "top-of-mind" when they are ready to buy. Peppers and Rogers said it best:

"Without customers, you don't have a business. You have a hobby."

In most businesses, "low hanging fruit" (the quick and easy deal) is a rarity. You can usually count on having to compete for every single sale. If you tilt the law of averages with a concerted effort to nurture clients, you will most certainly improve opportunities.

NURTURING BEGINS AT HOME

Negotiating courses have taught us during the past several decades that we must "make no concessions without personal gain". Sales reps are unaccustomed to giving a client or prospect something without reciprocity. However, on a cold call you are asking a potential customer who has never met you, or perhaps not even heard of you or your company, to grant you something—a sale, an appointment, or their time and attention—that you have not earned.

Unlike short-term fixes and quick sales, helping to solve a customer's business problem certainly helps to build long-term loyalty. Focus on your client's success—they will respond, and so will your reps.

Attitudes and behaviors toward sales and marketing change dramatically once reps see the results of nurturing.

Nurturing helps align a business's selling process with a client's buying process. Clients' skepticism will change once they realize that you are with them for the long haul and that you fully intend to assist them for the entire lifecycle of the purchase. But the process begins internally—with your sales and marketing staff. It begins with the realization that nurturing is a lifetime commitment.

THE KINDEST TOUCH OF ALL

One important factor in nurturing is the customer's actual perception. It does not matter what *you* believe constitutes a nurturing act—what does matter is how the other person perceives your actions. You must know a customer well enough to understand his or her values, passion and pains in order to make appropriate customer touches.

Naturally, what is perceived as a deposit by one person may well be perceived as a withdrawal by another.

Nurturing is a process designed to help you achieve positioning, differentiation, and influence. The key to its success is making certain that your customers receive the exact level of attention appropriate for them. The concept is similar to drip-irrigation in agriculture, the continual care the Chinese farmers gave to the black bamboo we discussed in Chapter 1.

In today's cynical world, it can be a struggle to prove that what you offer is unique—so, how can you prove it? Through a program of relevant and respectful customer touches that demonstrate you have more to offer than anyone else. This is particularly important when you are seeking high-profile clients.

Influential and affluent people are the prey of everyone seeking their business and all make the same claims: "We are the best. We are the greatest. We can do it all." The nurturing process does not shout those same tired messages. You differentiate yourself and your business by allowing the client to decide, on the basis of their interactions with you, that you provide a level of service and integrity that is truly different.

By regularly sending high-value communications to current and prospective clients you differentiate yourself as trustworthy. It is not difficult to do. You can touch customers through one of the most traditional, trusted, and readily available means available—the postal service.

Nurturing helps you sow the seeds of relationships simply by sending unique and valued messages to clients and customers on a regular basis. These can be anything from letters that offer tremendous value-added information to occasional humor.

GOOD THINGS COME TO THOSE WHO WAIT

How often you touch your clients and prospects depends on your relationship with them and the nature of your business. The touches should be far enough apart (five to six weeks) that they are not intrusive, but frequent enough to remain top-of-mind. Remember, watering too often drowns the plant. Insufficient watering causes the plant to wither from lack of care.

The pay-off comes over time. And that, in itself, is a point of differentiation. Not many salespeople are willing, or patient or persistent enough to communicate with a client for one to two years before making a sale. By the time that client is ready to buy, most competitors may have dropped from view and your name will be the one that is most familiar to the client.

I would like to introduce you to a patient man—Brian Ruh, a New York Life agent and investment advisor. He won New York Life's Agent of the Year award nine years running and has repeatedly produced in the top 50 with NYL nationwide. According to Brian, the secret of his success can be summarized in two words: Effective marketing.

Brian's "holy grail," as he calls it, is the nurturing process he used to establish lasting relationships by staying in touch with clients, prospects and, most importantly, centers of influence in the communities around his home office in New Holstein, Wisconsin. These are bankers, attorneys, accountants, and local officials who hold high-profile positions within the community and who have earned the trust of others.

Brian's ultimate challenge was to determine how to differentiate himself from competitors in order to gain and retain the attention of a core group of people hotly pursued by many others.

The nurturing process helped Brian learn how to strategically position himself in order to earn a place in the minds of clients, prospects, and centers of influence, and to manage solid ongoing relationships through a series of well-written, courteous mailings.

"Once the process is in place," says Brian, "it really is like drip-irrigating a garden."

Brian has been successfully using and refining the process of nurturing since he attended one of our workshops 10 years ago. He was skeptical about the process at first. The very idea of a prospective client calling him out of the blue to ask for an appointment seemed preposterous. By the end of the session, he was convinced. Brian returned home and put nurture marketing to work.

And it did work for him. "The problem in our business," Brian says, "is that so many times all we seem to be asking for is withdrawals, relentlessly pursuing 'low-hanging fruit' often well before we ever make any real deposits in the relationship. That would not work in a bank. It does not work anywhere else either. It certainly doesn't work in our business."

Brian's "deposits" in customer relationships begin with mailings, such as newsletters, publications, and concept papers. They are always personalized with a cover letter and always accompanied by attention-getting gifts and metaphorical enclosures. Brian calls them *trinkets*. The "withdrawals" begin only when quality face-to-face sessions are scheduled with clients.

He sometimes refers to his nurture program as "my personal, multiple contact process" because the program is devised to slowly, patiently, and persistently influence the client through many different touch-points.

Nurture marketing farming, can not be rushed. The real key to its success is patience. It is not always asking for the business up front. The approach should be respectful, relevant, and as much fun as you can make it. It should never be threatening.

In his mailings, Brian says, "I'm not showing my teeth, so to speak—just bringing value and letting them know I'm there. Behaving in such a way as to demonstrate what it would be like to work with me someday."

And do not think you must always write these letters yourself. Brian Ruh, for instance, leverages the wide range of resources that New York Life makes available to its agents. Your company might already have boiler-plate material you can customize—topical newsletters and whitepapers you can personalize with your photo and business address, and an appropriate, personalized cover letter. You can put your face on it. You can put your address and name on it and, with a simple commemorative stamp, you're appropriately positioning yourself.

Brian Ruh knows a bit about this. He routinely asks clients who call him "What prompted you to call me?" One prospect, now a client, proved the power of persistence when he answered, "Well Brian, you've been writing to me for four years and I was ready to talk."

Of course the phone does sometimes ring with surprises—you can have early returns for your effort. But reaching the level of awareness and trust needed to ensure an ongoing customer relationship can literally take months to years of patient, intelligent cultivation.

Research and experience show that people buy when they are ready to buy and not a moment before. Everyone has his or her own timetable for buying and in all likelihood it will not magically line up with your desired timetable for selling. Some clients may have a relatively short sales cycle; others, sometimes referred to as "slow adopters", can take months or years to decide to change a current service or product provider and then follow through with actually finding and choosing a new resource. It follows, therefore, that an increase in sales could be yours merely by actively cultivating and nurturing those slow adopters.

Think about it this way: as a sales opportunity ages, it is only natural that some will fall into the "sold" column of your competitors. Usually, however, the longer a prospect waits to buy, the less competition there is for their business. Reflect on the last time you were in a position to make a purchase and you took your sweet time contemplating it. Is it not true that the number of follow-up calls you received from vendors diminished as you extended your buying cycle?

To be more competitive, persist. To get the sale, be patient. Be the one who follows up with slow adopters. Better yet, keep your name in front of them on a regular basis so they will automatically call you when they are ready to buy!

Do not give up simply because the prospect did not accept your offer when you most needed the sale.

Take courage from the fact that as time passes, less disciplined competitors will almost always stop calling on a prospect too soon leaving a clearer field for you. They will fail to use strategies as simple as postcards, personalized letters, or even a well-scripted voicemail message. If you take a disciplined approach and put into place a long-term process of nurturing these slow adopters, they will think of you first when they are finally ready to buy.

Understand your clients. Be persistent. Have patience. These three rules would seem almost too easy to be true—but winners, like successful farmers, are *invariably* patient, persistent, and understand their clients.

It makes no difference what you are selling, how you get leads, or whether you are working for yourself, a small company, or a large corporation. In selling, as in farming, *kicking the tree has never been known to hasten ripening!*

Chapter III— Differentiate and Position

"If what is keeping your clients awake at night isn't keeping you awake all night, you're focusing on the wrong stuff"

Tom Peters

CONTENTS

WHO YOU GONNA' CALL?

Nurturing is not about smile therapy. It is about the kind of business therapy your customers need when their pain keeps them awake at night. But before they can turn to you for that therapy they need to know your position in the market and be sure you can cure what ails them. Now you have the opportunity to differentiate.

I like to tell a little tale to illustrate the importance of differentiation. I call it my spear doctor story.

You might wonder why anyone would need to know anything about a spear doctor these days. We rarely see spears today but back in ancient times the Greeks and the Macedonians went to war with them just as countries do with guns today. Now we call them javelins and the only place we throw them is in the summer Olympics.

Imagine that I am mowing the grass one day and, suddenly, a spear wings its way across my backyard fence and lodges in my chest. Unbeknownst to me, the neighbor's son next door is practicing for the Olympic javelin team. Suddenly, I have a pain in my chest and my awareness of spears has risen a hundred fold. Whom should I call for help?

There are a lot of general practitioners in the phone book, but I know I need a thoracic surgeon. Opening the Yellow Pages, I see an ad for a thoracic surgeon—not just any thoracic surgeon, but one who specializes in javelin removal. That surgeon is differentiated by the fact that I can confidently turn to him to remove the spear and relieve my pain, and restore my health. Suddenly among all the doctors I could possibly call, that surgeon is at the top of my mind.

I tell this story because it says a lot about pain and power. When we have a specific need in business, we rarely look for generalists in the business-to-business marketplace. We look for specialists who can help us solve our unique problem—one who can relieve our pain.

The time to be on the top of your customers' minds is when they need a specialist and you are remembered as the one with that specialty.

Too many businesses today have become commoditized by their customers. They compete strictly on price. If you can not differentiate yourself, or identify what is unique about yourself and your offering, then ultimately you are a commodity. You certainly do not want to become a commodity because, if the landscape of your market changes—and markets often change suddenly and dramatically—you will find yourself with nothing to sell.

THE UNIQUE SELLING PROPOSITION

Nothing defeats commoditization like a USP. USP is shorthand for "unique selling proposition." Most of us have one whether we know it or not. It is what makes us and our offering different.

If you want to see the power of a USP, take a look at retail. There are so many products and providers in the retail business that only the best survive—those with a USP that differentiates them from their competitors.

Nordstrom has been synonymous with high fashion and customer service since the Nordstrom family started its first shoe store in Seattle in 1901. Look at the power of that brand today.

A story circulated for a while about a lady who walked into one of their stores and said she wanted to return a set of tires her husband had purchased there. They told her they did not sell tires, but she insisted that her husband had purchased them at Nordstrom's—so they took the tires and returned her money.

Customer service is Nordstrom's USP. *Business Week* describes Nordstrom's as "customer service at its best." As a result, everyone nodded their heads and believed the story. Jim Nordstrom was asked if the story was true and he replied that he didn't get out to all the stores and so he didn't know; he added, however, "It sounds like the kind of stuff we do."

Your USP is what you do. It is what your business is known for. It is your reputation among your customers.

Companies such as Nordstrom differentiate themselves and find a niche with their customers.

When customers think of Nordstrom, they associate the store with outstanding customer service.

CUSTOMER EMPOWERMENT

Do you think your customers talk about you to others? When they talk about you, what do you think they say? What position does your business occupy in their minds? Have you told them lately?

Nurture marketing is a process of communicating over an extended period of time to build top-of-mind position in the minds of your customers. You and your company, through repeated touches that communicate your USP, will eventually be perceived as best-of-breed in your field.

Securing that position begins with differentiating yourself in the market and sowing the seeds of relationships by sending clients and prospects unique and valued messages on a regular basis. Brian Ruh, whom you met in an earlier chapter of this book, sometimes refers to his nurture marketing program as "my personal, multiple contact process."

Have you noticed how consumers today switch products on the most fleeting of whims? They can do it, you know, because the myriad number of product and service choices empowers them to do so. Customers want to be empowered. They want a positive customer experience. This is no secret. It is certainly no secret at Nordstrom. It was no secret to

Marshall Field or to Stanley Marcus. And customers are out there evangelizing their positive experience.

The biggest challenge for companies is reinforcing their USP with customers. Traditional advertising is undergoing transformation to web-based communications. However, pop-up blockers and on-demand media enable customers to avoid unwanted advertising. They make mockeries of advertising schedules. People now program their favorite television shows on TiVo or the VCR to watch later and fast-forward through the commercials. Spam filters and internet pop-up blockers further frustrate a business's attempts to advertise directly to customers.

If customers are blocking advertising, where are they going to get information about products and services if not through a systematic process of "dripping" the information on them through multiple channels?

Mention the words "customer empowerment" to marketers and most will shrink away from you like Dracula from light. Customer empowerment appears to them as the equivalent of driving a stake in the heart of marketing.

THE POWER OF POSITIONING

The Cancer Treatment Centers of America (CTCA) has one of the most identifiable USPs in healthcare today. For starters their name identifies their service offering. They treat cancer. CTCA does not cower in of the face of consumer empowerment. They embrace it in their many radio and TV ads, on their web site, and in the testimonials of their patients. They know all about customer empowerment, but because they are a healthcare organization, they call it "patient empowerment."

Patient Empowered Medicine is at the heart of CTCA's mission. In 1982, the mother of CTCA founder Richard J. Stephenson lost her life due to complications following treatment against transitional cell bladder cancer. The lessons he learned from her experience, coupled with six years of research into patient-centric healthcare, led to the creation of CTCA in 1988 in Zion, Illinois.

CTCA works to empower patients with information about their cancers and engage them directly with the medical staff to determine a course of treatment. At the heart of its offering is a focus on building patients' immunity through nutritional and spiritual approaches that complement traditional surgical, radiological, and chemotherapy treatments.

When Stephenson learned about the nurturing process he jumped at the concept's synergy with his own organization's inherently nurturing philosophy. Before Nurture Marketing came to CTCA, everyone requesting information from CTCA was contacted by an oncology information specialist (OIS). This individual possessed a deep knowledge of the different types of cancers, their treatment options, national and local support networks, insurance, and general healthcare issues. They would gather information from the callers, determine whether a caller was qualified and ready for treatment and, if so, enroll them in a program.

Those who were not ready or able to enroll would receive follow-up calls at later dates. But there was no systematic mechanism to ensure that the specialist would still be in touch with the patient at the time they were ready to make a decision. And the growing volume of calls was making it more and more difficult for the OIS staff to follow-up.

Following an initial Nurture Marketing consultation CTCA launched two carefully targeted nurturing programs—one for prospective patients and one for their caregivers. Data collected by the OIS staff was fed into a Microsoft Access database that was integrated with a simple Customer Relationship Management (CRM) program that automated the nurturing process.

Patients who had not committed to seek treatment and who were in danger of falling through the cracks of the old system were immediately assigned to the nurture marketing program. Very quickly, CTCA saw a return on investment. Their enrollment grew. Patient numbers improved each and every month as more patients were enrolled into plans that fit their needs. CTCA reported an improvement of nearly 10 percent in patient enrollments as a result of the nurturing program.

Patients who are interested but not ready for their program are automatically enrolled in CTCA's nurture marketing program. The OIS then begins to develop a personal relationship with each of them. Every few weeks, and only with the prospective patient's permission, some form of personal communication is sent from CTCA. Mailings often include nutritional information, analyses of new options for treatment, or materials to provide moral support.

The CTCA database is designed to identify those who qualify for treatment at CTCA and enable OIS specialists to work closely with the candidates to enroll. But for those who can not come to CTCA—either because their insurance will not cover treatment, or they do not wish to travel to a facility, or they are not ready to decide on a treatment program—the program allows an oncology specialist to stay in touch with them by sending additional information and directing them to other helpful resources where they can get their questions answered, their needs met, and still feel empowered through their interaction with CTCA.

"Essentially you can pitch another dime—which is the cost of nurturing—into the bucket and you're going to get a fantastic return," according to Jack Moore, CTCA's Chief Marketing Officer. Nurturing allows them to leverage their print and television advertising and follow up on the leads it generates. Nurturing extends involvement with the sales cycle.

But even if the financial returns were not there, CTCA would nurture because its sense of mission transcends business. Its primary focus is on the issues of life and death confronting cancer patients each day.

"If you know of something that could be empowering and would be useful, you've got an ethical imperative to find a way to tell people," says

Stephenson. "And that's what drives us to the nurture marketing process. It's what drives us in everything we do."

FINDING YOUR NICHE

Niche is not a bad thing. Once you know what niche you want you can very specifically target your customers. Naturally we can not be all things to all people but we can be something very important to certain people at certain times. Many of our customers initially have too broad a view of their marketplace when a focused view would benefit them greatly. I learned very early in my career that one of the most important things you can do to ensure your success is to focus on your customer's pain or problems. People will buy from you to relieve pain faster than to receive pleasure.

Carefully selecting your important clients is essential to a successful marketing and advertising campaign. As you move forward and begin to communicate with the market you'll find that customers are so scattered and diverse, and media advertising so expensive that, unless you are very clear about your targeted audience, you will not have enough money to drive enough touches to create top-of-mind awareness. Your marketing and advertising will be frittered away with little impact.

Once you've targeted your customers, you can then position yourself mentally—first to define your mission and goals internally and then to communicate that mission to your customers through marketing in order to position yourself in their minds.

Ultimately, that's the purpose of marketing. We must first identify who we are and determine what it is that we value. Then we must drive a process of communication that builds top-of-mind positioning as best-of-breed in the field.

If we do that, our name will come up automatically when our customers' pain keeps them awake at night.

Marketing must build top-of-mind awareness and a preference for our offering during a long buying cycle. If it doesn't do that, your efforts are wasted. As mentioned earlier, the time to be top-of-mind with a prospect is when they need help—not when we need sales.

For too long, businesses have gone along with the old sales theory that anyone could sell to anyone on a good day. In today's competitive market, a business must first differentiate itself and its offering from all others, and then develop a unique selling proposition it can communicate to its customers.

Ask yourself: What is it you are trying to do—attract new customers, retain old ones, or build alliances and relationships with centers of influence?

People want to deal with specialists. The era of the generalist is over. Find your niche. Once you have done that you can begin to nurture your customer relationships.

If you do not know exactly who you are or who you want to be in the eyes of your best clients and most desired prospects, you risk sending a bland, diluted message without meaning.

Positioning is the process of ensuring that clients and prospects perceive your product or service as superior relative to the competition. It is not about retooling your products or services. It is about reshaping how clients *perceive* your products or services.

Do your clients see you as a solution provider or a commodity purveyor? Do they see you as higher quality, technologically superior or lower priced?

Do you have a clear idea of what your clients actually want or need you to be?

Can you briefly articulate what is unique about your product or services within that frame?

Do you understand how your uniqueness specifically solves that particular client's or prospect's problems?

If clients and prospects can not instantly identify the differences between you and your competition then you haven't distinguished yourself. Effectively differentiating yourself is key to occupying your clients' top-of-mind.

Top-of-mind positioning, achieved through the consistent nurturing of clients, gives your company the competitive advantage. Nurturing clients with a consistently clear message can successfully strengthen relationships with your best clients and make your presence so strong that when a need arises your name and company automatically spring to mind. In other words your company becomes synonymous with an entire product or service category.

Success in business demands that your message be both brief and unambiguous to your most important constituencies. At the moment of truth, your message will be remembered if it has been crystal clear all along.

In today's competitive business environment, it is easy for your message to get sucked up into the cyclone of information and quickly forgotten— or worse, misinterpreted. If you sell X, Y, and Z, but your clients think of you only when they need X, then you will not get the call when they need Y or Z.

Remember, position yourself appropriately, differentiate yourself from your competitors, and be able to clearly state your business values, your products, and your services when meeting a client or prospect for the first time.

DIFFERENTIATE TO THE TOP

In what seems to be an eternally softening market, "A" level clients are your best hope for long-term survival. And under constant competitive pressure, it is a challenge to retain them, much less find time to identify, attract, persuade, and close new ones.

How do you do it?

You start by assessing the competition. Take a careful look at your competitors. Study the message they communicate in advertising, marketing materials, website, mass mailings, and brochures.

How do they differentiate themselves? What unique benefits do they offer?

Look at your product or service from every angle possible. What can you do that your competition does not or can not? Put yourself in a client's position and figure out how your product or service can solve their biggest challenge

Then assess yourself. Determine what separates your products or services from those of your competitors. What unique benefits do you offer? Do they really matter? Have you proven yourself to be better? Are your deliveries handled more efficiently and on time? Are your employees really more experienced? Are they friendlier? Are your contracts and policies genuinely more flexible? Are you rated at or near the top in your industry by independent authorities? Do you have a unique business history? Is it demonstrably easier to do business with you? Is your product built better? Easier to use? Easier to maintain? Clearly more cost effective? Consider asking your clients these very same questions and let them tell you how you are positioned with them.

Your goal in positioning is to emphasize what is truly unique about your company, play down any weaknesses, and defuse a competitor's strength. It is usually best to focus on a single benefit; clients simply will not believe that yours is the fastest, friendliest, and lowest priced offering in town all at the same time. Think—"Dominoes Delivers".

After you uncover your uniqueness, it is time to work that message into every corner of your market presence. The message needs to be everywhere you are: advertisements, marketing materials, website, brochures, phone hold messages, and e-mail. Clients need to "get" what you are all about. Instantly. The battle for top-of-mind is usually won with adroit positioning.

What a client can not name or frame, they can not claim.

A Unique Selling Proposition (USP) answers the fundamental question that every prospect asks: Why should I give my business to you instead of your competitor? If you can not articulate a USP, each sales rep is going to answer that fundamental question differently. Unless everyone in an organization answers that question the same way, and unless every communication with your clients includes the same consistent message, most marketing and contact efforts are a waste of money because clients end up confused rather than informed.

Incorporating your USP into your marketing messages (both written and verbal) gives clients and prospects a head-start by feeding them the right message at the right time in the right amount.

Ideally, a USP should describe your uniqueness and your ability to solve clients' perceived problems or pain points. Think about the memorable messages of successful brands over the years and the points of pain they addressed.

Remember the Clairol slogan "does she or doesn't she?" What was the point of pain there? Wasn't it that you'd be mortified if anybody knew you dyed your hair?

ELEVATE YOUR ELEVATOR SPEECH

It is not always possible for companies to sum up their USP in a single, short, memorable phrase. Your USP must, however, be as brief and to the point as possible.

Crafting an effective USP is not a simple task. Many companies retain outside help from marketing experts. The main challenge is to create a USP that fits your clients' perceptions, not yours. If you can identify their perceptions, then crafting your USP in-house is certainly possible.

One way of doing this is to host a client advisory board. Your best clients can be your best assets in helping you develop your USP. A client advisory board not only gives you a chance to show your appreciation to your best clients, it gives you the opportunity to ask why they prefer your company over your competitors, what you are doing right and what you are doing wrong, how you got their attention in the first place, and whether there are any other products or services they wish you provided.

Your clients may not tell you what you expected to hear but it is always valuable to hear what they are saying about you. Do not comment on the feedback or join the conversation—just listen. Record the information, evaluate the answers, and use that information as insight into developing your USP.

Once your USP positions your company, it is important that each individual on your team be able to briefly articulate that USP during the "elevator speech".

According to Geoffrey Moore, the term "elevator speech" was coined in the early days of marketing. In his book, *Crossing the Chasm,* Moore says "The best pitch was considered one that could explain an entire business proposition to someone in the time it took to ride an elevator a few floors." Thus, we call the pitch our "elevator speech".

Your elevator speech may become the most profitable 60 selling seconds you will have. It is your way of verbally communicating your USP to prospects you meet every day. Every elevator ride or chance meeting is an opportunity to differentiate your business. The best way to communicate your USP when you meet a prospect or client face-to-face is first to learn as much as you can about the client's own business and pain, and address your USP to their needs. Clients can not know what to expect or how to value a product or service until they can place it in a comparative context.

Typically, when a rep is asked about their business, they begin their answer with "I" or "we", and continue rambling on in that vein, never giving a thought to how they might address the concerns and issues of the potential client, or how to make their answer memorable. And if it takes more than a minute to get the message across, they have talked too much.

A good elevator speech is not about "you"—it is about them. It should describe ways to solve your clients' biggest problems or challenges and demonstrate what you would do to alleviate their pain.

Before delivering your elevator speech, however, ask the client about their business and their biggest business problem. Then tailor your speech to their business and their needs.

Start with the word "for," not I, and then identify their pain. You might begin with something similar to the following:

- For university help desk managers whose staff can not properly document a call, we... or I...

- For software developers who suffer from an overabundance of support calls, we... or I...

Wrap it up by articulating how your company can alleviate that specific pain. For example:

- For university help desk managers whose staff can not properly document a call, we offer a special writing workshop that teaches how to document calls efficiently and make the captured information more usable to their organizations.

- For software developers who suffer from an overabundance of support calls we develop crystal clear installation instructions, user manuals, and quick reference guides that maximize the users' out-of-box experience and cut the number of support calls in half.

Finally, marketing based on an undeliverable promise will fail. You must consistently deliver the goods.

Once your clients and prospects understand what differentiates your business from your competitors and know the benefits of doing business with you, naturally, you *must* keep your word. Otherwise, your efforts will have been wasted.

Chapter IV—
Ready, Aim, Target!

"Without customers, you don't have a business. You have a hobby."

Don Peppers & Martha Rogers

CONTENTS

Chapter IV: Ready, Aim, Target!

MESSENGER SERVICE

Once we move from the message itself to the delivery of the message, technology comes into play. Once you have articulated your USP, technology enables you to keep your differentiation top-of-mind with your customers, prospects and centers of influence. CRMs or simple contact managers facilitate management of continuous nurturing campaigns.

One of the most common tools on a salesperson's computer is the contact manager. Let me tell you about contact managers—they were designed as "sales gunslingers' tools" that have evolved into powerful customer relationship cultivation solutions.

The real purpose of contact managers is to put information at the fingertips of a producer. With a contact manager you not only keep demographic data but also idiosyncratic data, such as who likes hunting, or who prefers fishing—the personal information you learn about a client over time. The contact manager is where you find the e-mail addresses, office phone numbers, and home phone numbers of your clients.

A contact manager systemizes things. It does not automate them. It does not do work. It reminds you to do it. Some of the better ones have a nice spreadsheet and a text editor along with the address book and the calendar. Fundamentally, contact managers turn your producers into free-ranging gunslingers who have their office with them when they travel.

I was on the customer advisory board of ACT! when they introduced that product as one of the first contact managers on the market. When I saw it I thought I'd gone to heaven because, finally, there was a place to keep information. I would always know where it would be and would not have to wait until I returned to the office or have to rely on my memory.

Back then, I knew about nurturing and the importance of staying in touch with people. Here was an electronic to-do list that reminded me to call a client on her birthday. I could go into that scheduler and put it down. I no longer needed scraps of paper to remind me—I became a to-do freak.

I entered more and more reminders and every morning Act! would wake up and tell me what I had to do that day. Finally, about three months into it, it said "good morning Jim, you have 209 phone calls to make today." All I had was about an hour to spend on calls so, guess what? I discovered the Delete key.

My contact manager resumed its function as a big address book. But that is what it is supposed to be. A contact manager puts useful information into a format we can quickly access. But it does not automate anything.

To automate a nurture campaign, you need a relationship manager module. In the high-tech industry, they are commonly known as "customer relationship managers", or CRM for short.

Use of a relationship manager implies two things:

1) This is going to be a long term relationship. This is not just a contact. This is not a conquest. This is a relationship I am going to build. Therefore, the more information I gather over time, the more useful the tool is.

2) That I'm not a gunslinger anymore. A relationship manager not only has a contact manager in it, it also has a fulfillment center. A relationship manager implies that I've got an assistant who works on the inside at a desk in a fulfillment center while I am on the outside selling.

Let us imagine that I met you at a trade show, somewhere and determined you are a prospect I want to nurture but I know that you are at least a year away from making a purchase. A relationship manager allows me to put you into a stay-in-touch program.

With a relationship manager I can put you into a plan I'll call E6. First of all, what is an E? For this example, an E is someone who is probably a year or longer away from buying and E6 is a plan that is already written. It is designed to let us proactively market to the majority of prospects for a period as long as 24 months.

You might not come to my conscious mind again—however, I now have a program that will trigger every planned event. Whether I am sending you a letter, a voicemail, an e-mail, or a gift, I have built an action plan that will be in effect for 24 months. All I have to do is enter you into my software, key-in "E6" on the computer, and the automated touches begin.

My commands now move to my administrator's computer. Each day, all the administrator has to do is hit "go" and the computer instructs the administrator to load 91 letterhead, 20 second sheets, 14 thank-you cards, 21 birthday cards, 17 newsletter enclosure sheets, and 15 article cover notes—all in that order. The administrator loads the printer with the appropriate stock and hits print.

The computer finds name #1, reviews the action plan and selects the appropriate step, customizes it, personalizes it, prints it out, then seeks the next name. When printing is complete, all that is left to you to do is sign and mail the letters.

Think of what just happened there! We have a producer who does not want to be inside following up on all the touches to be made. Inside, we have an administrator taking care of the details, thereby freeing the producer to do what he or she does best—sell.

If we agree that the entire selling process is dependent on contacts and that "out of sight is out of mind" we realize that we now have a process to keep us in clear sight. The process depends on repetition to succeed—a repetition of contacts to earn you top-of-mind positioning. And we now have a computer handling the tasks that enable us to drive those repetitions.

Now, if I know you are not likely to buy during the next two years, it is not terribly productive for me to see you personally until then. But with an action plan that has been automated through a relationship manager, I can write to you during that period to keep renewing the acquaintance. When you are ready to buy, who will be at the top of your mind?

Since I have built a series of activities and automated a stay-in-touch plan, my job is very simple. When potential customers give me their business cards and their permission to communicate with them, I try to deduce from our conversation which action plan is appropriate for them. As soon as I key-in your name and designation as an E6, I do not have to consciously remember you anymore. The computer and my administrator will manage my communications to you. All I have to do is sign the letters.

TARGETING CUSTOMERS

Our most successful clients are those who micro-segment their marketplace to such a degree that they become Subject Matter Experts (SMEs) in their client's business. You need to specialize and know everything about your target marketplace. For example, Wes Snow of Ascendix sells software and services to a specific subset of the real estate market- the REIT or Real Estate Investment Trust companies and property managers exclusively.

Targeting simply means finding out enough about your customers to effectively align your sales process with their buying cycle. Clearly we can not automate our marketing process to do this until we have identified, categorized, and written an action plan for the customers we want to target.

Nurture marketing requires permission-based action plans that are tailored to your customers' sales cycles. It is not a one-size-fits-all program. Too many companies bet the farm on one-shot offerings designed to entice customers up front. So it should be no surprise to them when they get one-time bargain hunters who are only interested in finding the lowest price.

You have probably had customers like this. I know I have. They are the ones who are peering over the back fence in search of greener pastures during their conversation with you. And while they are wringing the lowest price out of you, harvesting the introductory offer, they continue searching for someone else's. Customers who are the easiest to get are often the hardest to keep and those who are the toughest to come by are often the ones who become your best long-term investments.

History shows it often costs five times as much to find a new customer as it does to keep an existing one happy. That is why smart organizations focus more of their resources on keeping and growing current customers and cultivating "A" prospects who are willing to give their proposals serious considerations.

They also persist with prospects they are confident will one day buy. It has been reported that 6 out of 10 prospects will turn you down four times before they make a purchase. Your "A" clients and "A" prospects are not likely to give your proposals serious attention until they have business needs—pain—that requires your expertise and enough exposure to remember you.

Customers operate on their own buying cycles and the only way you can ensure that you will you will be the one they remember when they are ready to buy is "to never be far away." That's what nurturing is all about.

Targeting begins with determining who your best clients are. Of course, they are the ones you want to nurture first.

In the farming metaphor, your database is analogous to your garden, and your clients and prospects are your plants and seeds. If you are like most, you probably enter the business cards of everyone you have met. You return from a trade show with a fist full of business cards and enter all that information into a contact manager. But when we talk about targeting, we are not talking only about following up on contacts we have made. We are talking about building relationships.

The targeting process begins by identifying the customers who could contribute the most to your success. It involves categorizing your current clients and prospects according to how well they help you meet the goals your have for your own business.

You might seek clients who represent the best match with your company's products or services, those with the greatest potential for growth, or those with whom you enjoy a certain type and quality of relationship. You might target clients by the amount of revenue earned from the client, the referral and testimonial value of a client, or by the length of their buying cycle.

THE "YOUR GUYS" CONCEPT

I believe I can say with confidence (since you are reading this book) that you are searching for ways to generate more sales or ways to prevent customer erosion. Perhaps you want to influence businesses that are neither customers nor prospects, but are centers of influence within your industry, or perhaps within your own staff. Whoever or whatever your target, you must identify it with precision.

For example, let us imagine that your focus is on customer retention. You want customer companies of a certain size, but if you can not target all of them you certainly want to target your A-level clients.

Once we identify the target customers, we can ask "Why do they buy? What is their motive?" We then want to determine whether the targeted customers' motives are seasonal, and if so, we will want to modify or adjust our action plans accordingly.

In business, as in farming, all seeds are not equal. It is a given in agriculture that some seeds simply will not germinate. The same applies to business—we recognize among all our customers and prospects that some will never become "A" level customers. We must carefully target those whom we wish to nurture—those who have the best chance of germinating and helping us prosper.

Husqvarna is a world-leading manufacturer of top-quality outdoor power equipment. Their products include chain saws, mowers, snow blowers, and tillers. Founded in Sweden in 1689, the company is one of the world leaders in outdoor power products for foresters and gardeners. It also has the distinction of being one of the oldest companies in the world.

How has Husqvarna prospered so long and so well? President Dave Zerfoss attributes much of the company's success to its long and healthy relationships with resellers in its ability to empower them in those relationships. "We identify with them so much and are involved with them so much. The very essence of our company is that these are 'our guys.' We feel that close to them," says Zerfoss.

Do you know who "your guys" are as unquestionably as Husqvarna knows theirs?

They are the ones who view you as a valued and dependable partner. They do not haggle relentlessly; they simply rely on you to deliver great value and superior results. Your best customers are the ones with whom you have built enduring relationships.

THE 80/20 RULE

Not all clients and prospects are equal. Focus your greatest nurturing efforts on your best.

When targeting clients and prospects, the challenge is to fix your eye first on those at the top of the food chain, but not malnourish those underneath.

It is difficult to abandon the notion that all clients deserve equal treatment, but given today's ferociously competitive climate, it is simply not practical or profitable to operate on that basis. The most effective businesses employ a process that allows them to systematically evaluate and prune their client roster on a regular basis.

In the early 1900s, Italian economist Vilfredo Pareto observed that 80 percent of the land in Italy was owned by 20 percent of the population. Since then, business has adopted the "Pareto Principle" (also referred to as the "80/20 Rule") to refer to the common phenomenon that 20 percent of customers usually account for 80 percent of business.

Using intuition and past experience, consider whom you would categorize as "A" clients; often they are your biggest clients. Think of "B's" as latent "A's". They possess "A" characteristics but have not yet matured or grown to a size meriting "A" level attention. "C" clients are what we call "bread and butter" customers; they demonstrate the affection and loyalty of an "A" and probably will never leave you, but they are not likely to ever generate the revenue or achieve the strategic value of an "A". With research we can usually figure out why.

Let's return to the farming metaphor to talk about "D" clients—think of them as weeds. Segment them, measure the return on your investment in them, and remove them when you realize they are not productive. If you do not, they will choke out the others in your garden.

Market segmentation is the process of grouping a market into smaller subgroups. Those subgroups might be demographic such as size, industry type, and revenue. They might be psychographic and have to do with a person's attitudes, lifestyle, or values. They could be geographic, or they might be behavioral—e.g., the person buys new equipment every three years.

Identifying your "A" clients is one of the vital steps you take as you prepare to nurture clients. It helps you crystallize your business objectives and hone in on the clients who will help you achieve them. You can not launch a drip-irrigation, nurture campaign that positions you "top-of-mind" among your best clients until you know who those clients are.

Here is an exercise:

List all your current clients and put a star next to the ones you consider to be "A's". When you think about "A" clients imagine which clients you would most like to clone and why. Then ask yourself why you consider those clients to be your best.

Revenue need not be your only consideration. "A" clients might also be the ones who pay on time, and doing business with them is easy and enjoyable. They might also frequently recommend you to others. "A" clients are typically those with whom you've shared a significant, long-lasting relationship based on mutual benefit and trust.

My co-author, Eric Rabinowitz, is an example of an "A" client. I met Eric in 1992 when he retained me to develop a marketing plan. By 1996, he had developed a team in-house that replicated what I taught. We stayed in touch and talked regularly about his own nurture process. Each month, I sent him letters and occasionally small gifts that dealt with the metaphor of nurturing. One such gift was an expensive orchid plant that Eric immediately assumed he had received by mistake. He called to tell me about the error. I responded that it was no mistake and that our team considered him to be one of our very best clients.

The orchid was a modest attempt to thank Eric for championing Nurture Marketing over the years. By then, he was an infrequent customer, but he regularly offered personal endorsements, testimonials, and direct referrals to my company. Every potential client Eric met became a client of mine. His referrals had become more valuable to me than many of my revenue clients. The strategic value and influence of an "A" customer can not be overestimated.

DETERMINING CLIENT VALUE

Naturally, the more information you have about a client or prospect the more accurately you will be able to forecast their potential ultimate value.

A client's ultimate net value is a combination of their actual revenue value and their lifetime strategic and endorsement value. Quantifying these values often requires savvy speculation.

Client information can be gathered through research—visiting the company's web site, collecting information through newspaper clipping services, Google/Yahoo, 10-K reports (public companies), press releases and internal publications, product literature, trade show materials, executive biographies, *Who's Who* listings, interviews, recruiting materials, and word of mouth.

With resources like these you can do everything from examining a company's mission statement and determining their general direction to finding out who the key players are and what the company's organizational structure is. Some companies offer an extensive listing of their clients online.

Major initiatives a company is currently undertaking, as well as issues or legal proceedings the company is facing, can be found online.

Look for hot trends or newly proposed government regulations in the industry that will affect the company positively or negatively. Seek company success stories, information on its finances, public statements about its future direction, and the kind of international relationships the company is building.

If you can not find information on the Internet call the company and request the information or ask to be put on a mailing list.

Unless the predictable, full life cycle, economic value of an existing average "A" client is quantified, it is virtually impossible to calculate the value of attracting new clients, or to determine the cost of retaining an existing client.

The ultimate net value (UNV) of a client is the sum of the following two components: lifetime cash value and strategic value. Lifetime cash value is measured in dollars. Strategic value, while also measured in dollars, has a qualitative component attached to it.

Lifetime Cash Value (LCV)

The LCV of an "A" client is calculated using the following two components:

1. Average annual revenue from a "A" client (REV)
2. Predictable life cycle in years (YEARS)

LCV = REV * YEARS

Average annual revenue from an "A" client

If an "A" client has been around for many years the calculation of lifetime cash value is straight forward. Add the total revenue for each year and divide by the number of years they remained a client. This will give you the average revenue per year of this client over their current lifetime. Multiply this average by the estimated number of life cycle years that you expect this client to have and this will give you the life time cash value. If you are unsure of the predictable life cycle years check your records, use your gut or research your competition.

If an "A" client has only been around a short time try this method. Look at the financial profiles on five similar "A" clients. Choose an "A" client that has been around a year (perhaps this client) and an "A" client that has been around for many years that may be approaching the end of their lifecycle. Choose three clients that are evenly distributed between your newest and oldest clients. Calculate the total revenue for each of these five clients and divide that total by the number of years they remained a client.

After you've calculated the average annual revenue for each "A" client, add the five calculated averages and divide by five which will result in the average annual revenue from an "A" client (REV). As before, multiple this average by the estimated number of life cycle years and this will give you the life time cash value. If this truly is a new "A" client this life time cash value calculation should be accurate.

Predictable life cycle in years

Look through your records to determine the average retention of a typical "A" client. If you have a relatively new company you may need to research the average life cycle of a typical "A" client. I've been successful asking business owners in similar businesses about their lifecycle experiences. (YEARS)

Example: If the average annual REV from your five "A" clients is $276,000 and YEARS is equal to 5.5 then your life time cash value for a typical "A" client is:

$1,518,000= $276,000 * 5.5

Strategic value

Strategic value is not as easy to quantify since it is based on the value of referrals, introductions, and endorsements from the client, as well as the value you place on their name recognition. Quantify what you can such as revenue from referrals and introductions that lead to a sale. Be aware that these sources, while not easily quantified, can easily transform a "B" client into an "A" client.

Once you determine the Ultimate Net Value (UNV) of a client you can start making decisions on how much you plan to spend to keep that client and to get prospects that behave like your "A" clients. How much would you spend to keep a client that generates $1,518,000 in revenue in 5.5 years?

Clients such as The Cancer Treatment Centers of America regularly provide testimonials and references. In the not-for-profit sector, CTCA possesses a "prestige value" that makes it easier to influence and gain top-of-mind with other research and treatment centers in that sector.

WHOM TO NURTURE, WHOM TO PRUNE

Once you have identified your "A" clients, take a moment to consider your "B's" or "next best" clients, and your "C's" or "bread and butter" clients.

What must that client do to move up or down one category? Where does the client fit into the market segment and what does the client most value about your business? If you can not find solid answers, ask yourself if your business would be better off without that client.

"B" clients are typically those whose revenue seems to be below potential but they have name recognition as well as potentially high strategic value and lifetime revenue value. They are also clients who respect you and your company's products or services.

"C" clients, remember, are your "bread and butter" clients regardless of whether they possess a high lifetime revenue value or strategic value.

"D" clients starve the rest. They are the ones who buy little, pay late, constantly haggle, change orders at the last minute, and frequently return items or ask for refunds for vague reasons. They demand customer service for questions that have already been asked and answered. Ask yourself if they might be costing you more than they are worth. They very likely are, and as you review your "D" list consider eliminating them from your list of customers you nurture.

Profiling your best clients not only helps you determine those you want to nurture and those you need to prune, it also helps you to segment and target viable prospects. Using the same criteria you used to segment your clients, grade your prospects "A", "B", "C", or "D". (We offer a tool, located in the Appendix of this book, to help you with this calculation).

Then make a commitment to nurture the "A's", "B's", and "C's". Weed out the "D's.

KNOW THY CLIENT

For many people a difficult question to answer is, "What aspect of doing business with me does this client most value?" If you can not answer that question, how can you possibly attract the types of new clients your business needs?

One way to learn the value you offer your clients is to ask them. Send a survey to all clients or call each "A" client personally. This is not only a great opportunity for a personal nurturing client touch, but clients are usually much more satisfied when they know that you truly care what they think of your company.

Whenever you receive feedback study it carefully. What are your "A" clients saying about you that your "B" and "C" clients aren't? Do you sense an opportunity with any of your "B" or "C" clients to take the relationship further and bump them up a category or two?

If a client is displeased, can the problem be resolved? Would a personal call or visit help? Could there be other clients who are unhappy about the same issue but did not mention it?

Are clients asking for a product or service you do not currently offer? It is almost always easier to add a new product or service than it is to find new clients, so determine how you could meet your best clients' needs.

We said earlier that market segmentation is the process of grouping a market into smaller subgroups based on demographic, psychographic, geographic, and behavioral variables. The way a particular market is segmented will be based on a number of variables unique to your product or service.

Demographic variables might include age, education, gender, income, occupation, and position. Psychographic variables might include attitudes, lifestyle, personality, and values. Geographic variables might include climate, region, and country. Behavioral variables might include brand loyalty, decision making unit, product use, product usage rate, and the buyer readiness stage.

Discover what your clients' major sources of anxiety are with regard to their business, their customers, and their lives. Capture the information when they tell you what keeps them awake at night. By alleviating those fears you will permanently etch a top-of-mind position with those clients.

A clear understanding of your clients' key emotional drivers will put you in a unique position to seize opportunities. It will also allow you to develop permission-based action plans with unique nurturing client touches that truly matter.

Chapter IV: Ready, Aim, Target!

Chapter V—
Drip, Drip, Drip

"He that can have patience,
can have what he will"

Benjamin Franklin

CONTENTS

Chapter V: Drip, Drip, Drip

A TREMENDOUS WHACK

Winston Churchill once said that when you have an important point to make you should not try to be subtle or clever. Use a pile driver. Hit the point once. Then come back and hit it again. Then hit it a third time—a tremendous whack.

We do not recommend that you whack customers but, like so many other words out of that old statesman's mouth, there is a lesson in what Churchill said. That is the rule of repetition. Repetition is what gets us remembered.

Realize that 50 percent of all prospecting attempts are aborted with the first "no". That means if a rep cold-calls you and you say "I'm not interested," there is a 50 percent chance that you will never hear from that rep again. Fifteen percent of the time that rep will contact you a second time and say, "I know you were busy when I was here before but I think we have something to talk about." You reply, "No" once again. Now, at this point, 65 percent of salespeople will give up. They are out of the game. Fourteen percent will come back a third time. By the fourth contact 90 percent of the salespeople will have given up. Ninety percent will never come back to that prospect you are calling on and yet all the research says you will not even be remembered until you have made 9 contacts.

When you are in a two-year buying cycle, you may need to make as many as 24 contacts to maintain a presence; however, if you are among the 90 percent who gave up, you would have quit after only four.

Let's say you are not a quitter. Say you have stayed with them through 12 to 24 contacts. Now, when the need arises and they are ready to buy, whom do they call?

It is a given that the brain generally chooses the path of least resistance. If my need is insurance, one side of my brain says, "You really ought to call the American Institute of Insurance Agencies and get a list of the 10 best agencies in Seattle." I know I should call all 10 of those agencies and obtain the names of their five most satisfied customers, call all 50 to get their ranking, and then decide whom to call.

However, I have been receiving mailings from Jerry for two years now. He seems to be patient. He seems nice enough. He is not rude and his mailings indicate he knows my issues. I understand his philosophy and I really do need to get this problem off my desk. What do you think I am going to do? Do I call Jerry, or am I going to place calls to all the other agencies?

KEEP ON KEEPING ON

The path of least resistance is the way CEOs solve problems.

I work with a group called Vistage (formerly TEC, the world's largest CEO membership organization). A few years ago, I met with members to learn how they choose new professional service providers such as an accountant or technology professional. They told me that they first call their best supplier when they have a need that they can not fill themselves. They might also call their Vistage colleagues and ask for personal referrals.

If they do not have a good relationship with their supplier and their friends can not offer referrals, they consistently turn to the expert who is most familiar to them.

That is where nurturing pays off.

A fourth alternative indicated by the CEOs is to turn to a big name—you have heard the saying, "No one has ever been fired recommending IBM." As a last resort, they turn to the Yellow Pages which they regard as a signboard for finding a bidder's list.

So think about it. Nurturing your "A" list clients puts you at the top of their minds—you are the one they call. Nurturing your "A" list prospects might place you third on their list, but once you do make a sale, it is easier for you to slip into that top slot on their list. And you never know when the visibility you gain through nurturing might put you on someone's referral list. However, you must communicate with the prospect repeatedly or you will not be on the list at all.

Once you have your action plan, it is time to get your hands dirty—it is time to set up a drip irrigation process. The actual practice of nurture marketing establishes a system through which customers and prospects are nourished with frequent high-value communications. We call them drips. The drip irrigation system is the key to communicating the right messages to the right people at the right time.

Wes Snow is the CEO of Ascendix Technologies, Texas-based providers of customer relationship management and sales force automation solutions. He has been practicing nurture marketing for so long he has become quite a spokesperson for it. The long process of cultivating a customer relationship, Wes tells me, is understandably difficult for salespeople. We are commissioned on today's sale, not tomorrow's. Inevitably, that drives our behavior and we stop persisting after we are told "no" three or four times. It simply is not in our DNA to "keep on keeping on."

The best way I know to keep on keeping on is to create and implement a strategic, nurturing plan.

PLAN ON IT

Once you have done your prep work, identified your best customers, found out why they remain loyal, what they wish you would stop doing, what their future buying plans are, and who has top-of-mind in that market place, you can create a strategic plan for keeping current customers and targeting new ones.

After studying your plan, ask yourself, "How many new customers can I absorb next year?" Rather than aiming for all you can get regardless of the consequences, narrow your wish list to an appropriate number to be cultivated.

Then ask yourself: If I concentrate on the "A's", do I really want to go after "B's" and "C's"? Identify how many new customers you want and whom you want to pursue in the next 12 months.

I recommend that if you know you need 12 new "A" clients next year, you put a hundred into your plan.

Know that statistically about 15 percent of your clients each year is up for grabs so if you want 12 new clients next year put 100 prospects into your plan and you are in the ballpark. I recommend you do this rather than start with a thousand. Big numbers get weighty and are difficult to manage. So start with a number that seems logical and doable.

After you've identified the 100 prospects you want to target, build an action plan to establish how you are going to stay in touch with them. Step 1 might be a letter of introduction saying, "I just want to write and introduce myself." Then, ask yourself what Step 2 should be and how quickly should it follow Step 1.

Your action plan, in simple terms, should state what you want to achieve and how you expect to achieve it. Give the plan a name. Identify the clients you are targeting, state the desired outcome, and then specify each of the steps along the way (see the sample in Figure 1). We recommend laying it all out as you see here—in columns on sheets of paper. Allow one row for each step in the plan. We strongly recommend a 12-step plan. Remember, it will take nine contacts before you begin to make an impression. (See the Appendix for sample letters and scripts to accompany this plan.)

Figure 1

ACTION PLAN

GENERIC PROSPECTING – B TO B EXECUTIVE

Purpose: Ensure Top-of-Mind Positioning

STEP	DAYS	ACTIVITY	DESCRIPTION	ENCLOSURE
Step 1	0	Letter	Introduction	Brochure
Step 2	15	Letter	Gift/Offer	Book Summary
Step 3	40	Letter	Positioning	Crystal Ball
Step 4	15	Letter	Gift	Shredded Money
Step 5	15	Invitation	Invitation	
Step 6	5	Phone Call	Follow-up	
Step 7	20	Letter	Briefing Highlights	CD recording of the briefing
Step 8	7	Phone Call	After Event Follow-up	
Step 9	30	e-mail	Article of Interest	Link to your website
Step 10	30	Letter	List Letter	Transformation Article
Step 11	30	Letter	Paper-Solving Chief Pain	White Paper
Step 12	Seasonal	Greeting	Donation	Charity Card

In the first column, put down a number for each step. In the second column, list the number of days between each contact. For example the number of days between Step 1 and Step 2 is 15 and the number of days between Step 2 and Step 3 is 40. In the third column, identify what that activity will be— a phone call, e-mail, letter correspondence, or an invitation. In the fourth, briefly describe the activity and in the fifth column, identify the enclosure you will send.

Figure 2

BUDGET ENCLOSURES

Step	Description	Enclosure	# of Contacts	Enc. Cost	Total

Paper, Packaging, Envelopes

Step	Descript.	# of Contacts	Paper $	Env. $	Spec. Pkg. $	Other $	Total $

Once you have your plan together it is easy to budget using a form like the one in Figure 2. All you have to do is identify your "cost items" at each step and the number of items you'll be sending. Then total the amounts to get a good ballpark estimate of your nurture plan investment.

Once again, enumerate your steps. Write a short description of each one, identify the enclosure you'll include, the number of contacts, and the cost of the enclosure or dimensional metaphor. For example:

- Step: 1
- Description: Positioning Letter
- Enclosure: Crystal Ball
- Contacts: 50 prospects on your list
- Enclosure Cost: $2.00 each
- Total = $2.00 * 50 = $100.00

Your sheet should look like the one in Figure 2 but with your numbers filled in to show your cost per step. To get a true picture, you will need to factor-in the costs of paper, envelopes, packaging, postage, and other costs of mailing. Do the math. Total it and you have your budget for the plan. Now you are ready to drip!

WHAT IS DRIP IRRIGATION?

Good customers expect you to keep in touch. It is OK to occasionally tell them about a neat idea or new product, but be sensitive to their tolerance for contact.

Make sure that each contact is appropriate to the actual relationship-level you have attained. The one-to-one tools in CRM software solutions allow you to develop a learning relationship. Based upon information your prospects provide and products about which they inquire or purchase, you can attach or provide a link to key articles or Web sites that expand their knowledge in an area you know to be of interest.

Birthdays and significant holidays provide great occasions to make use of the versatility and intimacy of email to send an appropriate sentiment. By automating an annual nurture action plan, you can delegate the memory and even the creation of each event and gain the reputation as someone who cares and knows how to stay in touch.

I have observed four types of in-touch campaigns commonly used by businesses: One-Shots, Wave Campaigns, Triggered Campaigns, and Drip Irrigation Campaigns. All are expensive and time-consuming to implement but only Drip Irrigation promises substantial and measurable return on the investment.

One-Shots are common and are almost always centered on a single special event like a new product introduction, golf outing or client appreciation breakfast. They are planned months and even years in advance and, although they are certainly appreciated by the 10 or 20 percent who actually attend, they are not a very effective relationship cultivation process.

Wave Campaigns typically involve a series of letters (usually three) followed by a phone call seeking an appointment. They can shake out very low hanging fruit, but they are rarely educational or even informational. At times, too, the wave can seem inappropriate and sometimes manipulative to good prospects.

Triggered Campaigns are One-Shots that are triggered by an event. For example, the computer notices a measured reduction in contacts from certain customers to you so it triggers a personal phone call, a personalized letter, or an email that touches base and seeks an update on status. It is an intelligent, but still isolated, event. It does not nurture a relationship.

Drip Irrigation Campaigns are intended to cultivate awareness, interest, and loyalty over time using the power of repetition and permission-based communications. It allows you to pamper your best customers, and introduce and educate new clients to your market positioning and to your specific value and differentiation.

A true client-nurturing approach attempts to optimize the value of those relationships over their full life cycles (which can last decades if managed appropriately). Nurturing might contain both wave contact points as well as triggered events such as birthdays or client anniversary dates. Nurturing implies an intention to be of such genuine value to each client that their loyalty is not only easier to obtain, it is also in the client's best interest.

By using the permission gained by a purchase or an inquiry, simple technology allows you to convert initial interest into a full-blown dialogue and to automate much of the process. One way to start something is simply to let customers or prospects who visit your Web site indicate whether they would like to receive additional information.

Once the client opts in, your database is updated automatically. If you are using e-mail as your gardening tool, the message can contain your URL which can automatically launch your Web site, a new PowerPoint presentation, a demonstration, or a video. Be creative. Customers and prospects will be impressed.

Technology, software, and the Internet have joined together to let us drip irrigate our customers and prospects like the valued cash producing plants in a garden.

In an information blizzard, reaching and maintaining awareness and preference among your most important customers becomes more difficult, but even more vital than before.

Prospects and key contacts at existing clients can disappear suddenly as companies reorganize. This makes it especially important for you to stay in contact with your network of key customers, business friends, and industry colleagues. If you're dealing with just one key person and that person leaves, you're likely to be left out in the cold when a replacement is brought in.

Prospects present the same challenge especially in any business that has a long buying cycle. A good way to overcome these problems is to proactively stay in contact with people before they make a change and give them compelling reasons to stay in touch with you if and when they do move.

Keeping in touch today is always a permission-based activity and few things seem to earn permission to cultivate a client's loyalty better than knowledge-based interactions. Keeping your client touches personal, relevant, and even anticipated is necessary. Customers need to know that we appreciate, understand, and truly serve them.

A good drip marketing program lets you keep on keeping on in an automatic, systematic way. The key is to craft client touches that get remembered.

How do you do it?

CLIENT TOUCHES THAT COUNT

"It begins with your intentions," says George Nordhaus, founder and chairman of IMMS and Group 500 insurance marketing and management services. "If you really care about the individuals you serve, then take care to create reasons to be in touch with them."

Even in today's information-heavy environment, sending brief tidbits of relevant news and industry insight will, over time, create top-of-mind positioning.

New York Life's Brian Ruh commemorates each client's annual business relationship anniversary with an innovative and unusual touch. Using imaginative yet inexpensive desktop-publishing software, Brian's staff prints out an attractive one-page newsletter-like document that highlights key events that happened on that date throughout history. The newsletter focuses on the key happenings, people, and comparative pricing of common objects from then until now.

Each year on Valentine's Day, Bob Valentine, president of Seattle-based printing leader Valco Graphics, produces an elegant Valentine greeting and sends it to his best customers with a note that says:

"With a name like mine and customers like you, every day really is Valentine's Day."

The valentine is not only a thoughtful greeting, it stands as an example of the quality of work Valentine's company produces. Valentine sends out another thoughtful example later in the spring. At the peak of tulip season he sends his "A" clients three dozen of the freshest, most colorful tulips he can find and includes a brief note that reads,

"Just celebrating the colors of spring.
Your friend, Bob Valentine."

Finally, when the weather heats up in the summer, Valentine has his sales reps hand-deliver logo-sleeved Dove bars to every single employee at every single one of his best clients.

BANISH THE BULK

You are probably thinking, "Sure, it is easy enough for a printer with a name like Valentine to come up with a card on Valentine's Day, but how can I express the appreciation, respect, and affection I feel for my best customers?"

It is easier than you might imagine. All it takes is an intention to mold stronger ties with key individuals, a willing administrator to help with fulfillment tasks, and time and patience to sit down and write a few simple love letters.

But there are a few rules to keep in mind.

First, know that one of the deadliest things you can do if you are trying to reach a CEO or CFO is to send them something in an envelope with bulk postage on it.

Second, know that if it has a label on it there is a better than 60 percent chance that it will be thrown out without ever being opened. If it has any teaser copy on the outside there's a better than 88 percent chance of it being thrown away unopened.

It is not that the people to whom you are sending mail dislike advertising; it is that they get so much of it. If prospects can readily identify your message as bulk mail they will save themselves a second and simply not open it. And believe me, executives will take advantage of every second they can save.

Basically the rule is, if you want them to look at your communications, it should not have the appearance of junk mail. If it does, you are wasting one-half to two-thirds of your budget for a direct mail campaign.

Here is my tip: Keep a piece of junk mail that you have received and tape it to the top of your desk. Each time you prepare your campaign mailings, take a look at that piece of junk mail—you will certainly want to avoid its tell-tale signs of an easy throw-away,

Here are our 10 rules for avoiding the look of junk mail:

- Never use a window envelope.
- Always use a first-class commemorative stamp.
- Use quality paper and envelopes.
- Print the address directly on a standard envelope.
- Use your logo.
- Include a relevant trinket or small gift.
- Always hand-sign your letters using blue ink.
- Boxes, FedEx, lumpy mail (with trinkets inside) and 8X10 envelopes get opened. Use them.
- Instruct your post office NOT to barcode your mail (they may do this automatically even though your mail is already stamped). Mail with barcodes looks like bulk mail.
- Put your own name on the mailing list so you can see the finished result (as it appears when the client receives it).

HONESTY IS THE BEST POLICY

Nurturing is the beginning of a relationship, not a one-night-stand. With a one-night stand you do not have to tell the truth because if you are not coming back, you can say anything you please. When you embark upon a nurture program, you make a commitment to be honest. Remember, you will be coming back to that prospect again and again, and eventually, truth will be known.

You've seen those ads in the paper that say "make money at home addressing envelopes." People set themselves up with a list of addresses, a stack of envelopes, some post-it notes and stamps, and they make an assembly line. First they grab the letter then they look for the first name on the mailing list and it says James Bronson so they attach a Post-it note and write "Dear James, check this out. It looks great.—J." Then they stick it to a page that looks like newsprint, stuff it in an envelope, address it, add a stamp, and carry it off to the mailbox.

You receive it. There is no return address so you can not find out who sent it. Are you going to open it? You must because for all you know there might be a check inside. But what do you find? You find a page printed on newsprint. On one side, there are stock tables that make it look like something from The Wall Street Journal. The other side is all advertorial. But there is that Post-it note that says, "Check this out", and is signed by "J". So you ask yourself, "Who is 'J'?" You mentally list all the J's you know—then, finally, you read it.

Curiosity kills the cat. It drags you into the copy. If you target properly, it does work. That is the strategy of bulk mail.

But how deceptive! It is a lie and that is a terrible way to start a relationship. It is like saying on your first date, "I lied to you to get the date but I promise I'll never lie to you again."

If you want a relationship, you might as well start out with the truth and stay with the truth because sooner or later they are going to know the truth. And if that is not what they thought it was, you will lose them and you will have wasted much time and money in the process.

Another point to remember is that repetition is dangerous if you repeat the wrong message. I know many salespeople who allow designers to prepare their marketing communications with the unfortunate result of having created a false image and expectations that can not be fulfilled. Inevitably, it fails. It fails because people are generally intelligent enough to see through the gloss. In relationship marketing, where buying cycles are long, it is important to be what you are and to communicate a truthful message.

That is why targeting is paramount. We can not serve everyone well but some of us do offer superior service in certain segments of the market.

THE WRITE STUFF

The more you know about a customer, the better your chances of composing a letter that addresses that customer's needs. Consider the person's education, occupation and position within the company, his experience, anxieties and fears, attitude and motivation, environment, and reading level.

The busier a person, the more likely he or she will quickly scan your letter instead of thoroughly reading it. Make sure your main point is stated succinctly.

An effective introductory paragraph compels a reader to continue reading. Try something other than a predictable beginning (It was a pleasure speaking with you yesterday...). Instead, ask a question you will answer later in the letter or relate a human interest story you have read or recently heard. You could address a business challenge you know they are facing, or invite them to an event.

The body of the letter should contain information that is useful and relevant to the reader. It helps if you have a very clear goal in mind for the communication. Make your point simply and eloquently.

Ask for help with your letters. We all have untapped resources in our offices—people with excellent command of English and a desire to help. Involving people in your organization will help you write a better letter and is a great way of teaching others in your office what you are doing so that they develop an appreciation for nurturing and marketing your organization.

eNURTURING

E-mail gives you "24/7" access to your clients and prospects, but it is something that must be used with caution. Why? One word: Spam.

E-mail is a natural fit with nurturing because it is so easy to schedule and manage electronically. But beware. Spam is toxic. Unhappy recipients are likely to block you forever. Permission-based marketing is the only strategy to use when you go electronic. Your clients and some prospects really do want to hear from you, but they have a "contact tolerance level," especially when it comes to e-mail.

E-mail is a great way of keeping in touch with current clients, but is potentially poison when prospecting. If you do not yet have a relationship with a prospect, e-mail is almost always perceived as SPAM. An e-mail campaign should not be considered unless you have established relationships with the recipients. When embarking upon an e-mail campaign, it is important to test each step within a campaign. Carefully select a sensitive and friendly group to evaluate an idea before launching it to the world.

When using e-mail to nurture customers, make sure your messages are always relevant, positive, and interactive. Always include an "opt-out" that allows the recipient to control communications with you, especially for those suffering from information overload.

Mixed media works best. Supplement e-mail communications with postal mail and telephone calls.

THE SECRET IMPORTANCE OF STUFF

Most of us receive a myriad of items through the mail each day: junk mail, bills, checks, and items that catch our attention because of their lumpy envelopes. If you are like I am, junk mail gets tossed automatically. Bills get our attention and we open them because we have little choice. Checks make us smile and we quickly open those. And the lumpy envelopes? I am betting you open those, too! Items in lumpy envelopes pique a person's curiosity. They are irresistible—we want to see what is inside. Chances are, that is true of your customers, too.

Relevant, intelligent, appropriate enclosures (we call them "dimensional metaphors" around the Nurture Institute) ensure your mailings get attention. But to extend the recipient's attention, enclosures must have a relevant association with the specific point you are trying to make. The connection is made with metaphors.

What is a metaphor? Simply put, a metaphor draws a comparison between two objects or ideas to make them easier to understand, like the comparison of your customers to plants in your garden. Metaphors have a way of triggering previous experiences and, therefore, creating memorable associations. If you need ideas for metaphors, visit our website at www.nurtureinstitute.com.

Metaphors are ubiquitous. We use them in our daily conversations. We find them in literature, music, art—in short, we use metaphors wherever vivid imagery is needed to illustrate a point. In this book, for example, we use the metaphor of farming to illustrate nurture marketing and the process of "cultivating" customers.

Metaphors are essential in nurturing communications. Effective metaphors connect the enclosure and the message with relevance and impact. The enclosure, or "dimensional metaphor", makes the envelope lumpy, giving it a third dimension that, in turn, piques the recipient's curiosity and ensures that the letter will be opened.

Dimensional metaphors can be both informational and fun. Examples of informational metaphors are:

- Pages from a magazine article relevant to your customer (You could attach a personal note that says, "When I read this article I thought of you.")

- 21 ways to solve a particular problem

- An information white paper

- Any book or summary that solves a problem that you know your clients have.

Everyone wants to have a little fun, and interspersing your serious letters with some fun is almost always well-received. Examples of fun metaphors are:

- Crystal balls (Wish you could see the future?)

- Worry dolls (Let us handle you worries)

- Small metal tools (Having the right tool for the right job is the only way to succeed and we are the right tool)

- Squishy brains (Let us be your second brain)

Adding dimension to an e-mail requires more creativity on the part of the sender, and there are also courtesy protocols that one must observe:

- Send e-mail only to customers and prospects who have given their permission to receive your communications. SPAM is illegal, and since it is rarely read by the recipient, it is futile.

- It is preferable to send e-mail to prospects and customers only after several direct mail correspondences those who know you or your company.

- Include a link to a website of interest— remember to include reasons for which you feel the site would be worthwhile to visit.

- Avoid attachments since many SPAM filters automatically delete e-mails with attachments or flag them as suspicious or undesirable.

Ascendix Technologies uses a variety of powerful metaphorical enclosures in mailings to prospects once it identified its vertical niche as real estate and finance. Ascendix follows the micro-targeting with a drip campaign of nurturing communications.

Their mailings include trinkets such as paper weights, letter openers, Magic '8' Balls, toy tools, and Guatemalan worry dolls. Each dimensional metaphor is designed to distinguish the Ascendix communication from all other mail, capture the attention of the reader, and finally imprint Ascendix's brand and message on the mind of the reader—e.g., the worry doll is accompanied by a message that asks what was keeping the recipient up at night and suggests that Ascendix's solutions would remove the worry.

Avoid sending enclosures bearing your logo. As Ascendix CEO Wes Snow says, "This is all about them, not us." The Ascendix message is sent on a monthly basis and is targeted to Real Estate Investment Trusts and property managers. "I'm seeing the fruits of our labor. "It's amazing", says Wes. "We are realizing the fruit of a well-fertilized and well-watered crop called real estate."

Chapter V: Drip, Drip, Drip

Chapter VI—The Technology It Takes

"I have a simple but strong belief. The most meaningful way to differentiate your company from your competition, the best way to put distance between you and the crowd, is to do an outstanding job with information. How you gather, manage and use information will determine whether you win or lose."

Bill Gates

CONTENTS

THE WAVE OF CHANGE

We need technology to ride the wave of nurturing lifelong customer relationships.

Because the only business assets of any real value are the awareness, esteem, and loyalty of our customers we must leverage the power of today's technology to effectively stay in touch with them.

Current software products have the ability to use automated processes to create drip irrigation systems that automatically generate the letters and call scripts needed to execute specific plans for specific audiences. Properly set up, they ensure that the right information is always sent to the right prospect at the right time.

Databases give us the opportunity to customize templates with information that is tailored to fit the needs of clients. A good database program allows us to readily identify who our customers are and how we will communicate with them.

By using databases effectively you will discover new ways to connect your inside people to information relevant to people outside your organization. Whether it is salespeople to customer, administrator to salespeople, or customers to company you will realize that the key to managing relationships lies with information management and communications.

Imagine a marketplace in which you target a wide variety of prospects. When you sell to operations personnel you talk about efficiency and the time saved by using your product. The operations people receive a letter every four weeks for six months followed by a personal phone call. When you sell to corporate management you talk about competitive advantages and bottom-line performance. Corporate managers receive a letter every six weeks for eight months.

An automated system of nurturing keeps your message in front of the prospect professionally, intelligently, and persistently to help you attain the top-of-mind awareness you are seeking. It also uses your personal message to influence the prospect to think of your product in a positive light.

DON'T HESITATE. AUTOMATE!

If you have not already begun to automate your sales processes, now is the time to start.

Automated processes allow you to maintain regular contact with prospects, clients, alliances, and centers of influence with campaigns of intelligent, relevant, and useful letters, notes, and e-mail.

Powerful support tools such as software-driven marketing encyclopedias assist agents in creating sales presentations that incorporate the most up-to-date marketing information.

Opportunity management systems deliver a treasure trove of information on qualified prospects. Team-selling solutions combine and leverage the efforts of reps, marketing, and service staff, as well as customer support teams to provide fast, clean solutions.

Proposal automation ensures that the format, content, and context of each proposal is designed quickly and persuades intentionally every time.

Product and pricing tools help customize solutions on the spot.

If you haven't taken the technology leap here are just a few of the tangible benefits you are missing:

- Improved market coverage. Technology lets you improve market penetration and sales effectiveness intelligently and rapidly.

- Better analyses. Technology rationalizes the data in client information files and makes it easier to understand and use.

- Elimination of redundant efforts. Real savings develop from the elimination of steps in the sales process that do not add value.

- Improved efficiencies. Immediate savings will be realized from automating manual processes such as client follow-up and education.

- Higher productivity. Improvement in order entry and solution configuration reduces entry errors and boosts productivity.

MAKING CONNECTIONS

At the heart of the nurturing process is a central drip irrigation program that automatically follows up on contacts made with prospects. This process allows reps to begin to network differently—both inside and outside your company.

Automated drip irrigation requires only one member of your office personnel, generally an administrative assistant, to print the letters and the call scripts. The system inherently makes sales people more productive by freeing them to do what they do best—sell.

Once information is automated by an action plan for managing customer contacts, reps have the right to decide how heavily they need to be involved in those contacts. Most sales pros would rather be out selling.

No salesperson should be without a notebook computer. When you equip reps with notebooks or PDAs to use in the field, you give them the opportunity to use electronic software tools such as CRM programs. As salespeople utilize advanced technological tools to do their jobs it changes the way they work. But then synchronization becomes very important.

Let me give you an example:

If I'm working from home and want to put a prospect into an action plan, or if I'm working from a hotel and have the card of a person I want to assign to an action plan, modern technology lets me link to my computer wirelessly, log into my corporate system, hit auto-sync, and synchronize the database on my computer (the one with the new data) with the master database in the office. The next morning when the administrator comes in and runs the action plan, that prospect will be included.

WHAT IS CRM?

Customer Relationship Management (CRM) systems have become one of the fastest growing investments in the sales and marketing arena.

CRM itself has garnered a top-of-mind position with CEOs across the globe as they learn to embrace the necessity of effectively managing critical relationships at all levels of the enterprise. What is more vital to an organization's well-being than its ability to attract and retain key customers? The major benefit CRM provides is the ability to systematize the attraction and retention process. It is also why CRM has achieved a core position in the technology infrastructure of the enterprise.

Today's CRM technology is dramatically different from yesterday's technology. Only a few years ago when I used the expression "CRM" in a meeting I got a lot of frowns and blank stares. Old-school CRM software products did little more than add a power cord to the Rolodex. About all you could do was look up a client's telephone number and that was often easier to do directly from the Rolodex.

In the old days when customer information was tucked away in filing cabinets or sitting on desktop computers in individual departments you had a lot of valuable information that was not accessible to marketers. The people putting together marketing campaigns could work from demographics and the occasional sales report. They could study information on trends but marketers had no real access to data that would give them a comprehensive 360° view of the customer. Databases and CRM have radically changed our ability to access this data.

Centralized databases that could be accessed across a network now give them the ability not only to look at the customers but to search, sort, and get answers to key questions that often remained unanswered in the old days.

Today, you can instantly identify your best customers by calling up information that shows who placed orders topping $500,000 last year and who pays on time. You can enter prospects and their information will be automatically updated with order data when they actually become a customer. You can segment your market and target your customers by any number of criteria that you specify—annual sales, number of employees, position in the industry. And you can get all this information from a single touch on the keyboard.

CRM brings all that data together, sorts it, generates reports, and provides tools to the marketing department to analyze the data, create campaigns around it, budget those campaigns, track their success, and personalize and individualize the customer relationship.

For a glimpse at how CRM technology can transform a business, look at Amazon.com. If you've ordered books, CDs, or videos through Amazon's online store, you know that the next time you come back to the site it remembers who you are and what you ordered. Amazon says, "Hello Sue. Based on your recent orders, we have some recommendations of new books we think you might like."

Amazon revolutionized online retail marketing with that concept. Amazon.com showed CEOs how fast a competitor could change the face of an industry with the power of technology.

Everywhere today the Internet is spilling over with web sites that allow end users to enhance their client experience. They can perform transactions and track orders, review products, and register complaints. Customers tend to be more satisfied, costs are driven down, and new revenue opportunities are continuously exposed.

WHAT CRM CAN AND CAN NOT DO

Sometimes I think CRM is misnamed. It should be renamed *CRDM* - Customer Relationship Data Management. Software doesn't manage a relationship; it manages data. People manage relationships.

Someone once defined a relationship as the measure of the quality and quantity of the contacts between two parties. CRM only gives you the potential for positive contacts. It doesn't give you any more time. It doesn't change personalities (for example, phone phobia or any other reason why people do not stay in touch).

The one process CRM can not solve is the quality and demeanor of interpersonal communication. Although technology sets the perfect stage for communication to take place it can not replace the need for human-to-human exchange. That is the role of nurture marketing.

If you're truly intent on managing your customer relationships, nurturing should be at the heart of what you do with CRM. Use the technology to manage a nurture campaign and to generate the words, letters, notes, and strategic interactions needed to stay in touch with customers. These can communicate your vision, mission, and purpose. Technology ensures that the activities are only a mouse click away from being done but, in the end, it will be the level of client intimacy a company provides that determines whether its CRM system will succeed or simply exist.

The ability to stand out by staying in touch remains the critical step and the necessary agent for true relationship management.

Nurturing is not technology; technology is a tool to facilitate the marketing process (tracking, measurement, coordination, and management). You can nurture clients without software, but you can not do it indefinitely. You will eventually run out of memory and time.

You've seen Jeff Foxworthy's comedy routine, "You know you're a redneck if..." What makes that so funny is that we can all recognize ourselves. I want to advance my own variation on that theme. I call it "you know you need technology to nurture if..."

- You plan on having multiple action plans.

- You have more than 100 clients whom you plan to nurture.

- You start a new client or prospect in a plan and want to ensure they are contacted every step of the way.

- You want to use different messages to nurture multiple constituency groups.

FIRST STEPS

CRM software is here to stay. Prices are down to the point where almost anyone can afford it. Software not only lets you automate, it provides templates to help you do it.

Technology seemingly makes the process so easy that you run the risk of getting carried away with it.

It is an amazing phenomenon. Many people have said, "Let's get it all done at once. Let's get all of our prospects and all of our customers in there. Let's send letters to the centers of influence and get back in touch with old customers or lost customers. We'll build all the databases and all the action plans. We'll get all the letters written, all our people trained, and load everything in."

I can tell you that if you start on a scale that grand, you will never get it done!

I recommend starting with your 20 most important customers and your 20 most important prospects and get the first four drips into the mail to them. Track the feedback and you will find out just how powerful nurturing is. You will find that people can not resist this stuff.

When you start personally writing to customers, your customers will treat it personally. I always say if you treat it like junk at your end, they will treat it like junk at their end. Use the tools given in your CRM program to monitor and budget your program. I ask CEOs, "If you do not know how much a client is worth to you, how do you know how much you would be willing to spend to get one?"

In an automated nurturing system you can measure it to the penny. For instance, if I put you into an action plan, I can measure how much every one of those drips costs. I know that this one with the audio CD enclosure costs $5.00 and that the one with the brochure costs $1.50.

Using software I can append that information to each of those drips and the software will keep a running total of those investments for me. If I run a report, it will tell me at any given moment how much I've invested in a relationship. I can then start making decisions based on the results I get from the overall project.

I can learn that by the time I've invested $2,500, I've got 50 percent of the rate of return I wanted. I can see who has responded and who has not. If a customer has not responded by that level I may very well decide to drop them. But if I do not track investment and rate of return, I've got no way of knowing.

When I know how much I am spending and how much I am getting back I can plan and budget. Let's say that by the fifth drip 12 percent of the people we are nurturing have made some level of contact with us and by the 11th drip we have 21 percent of the clients we targeted. Next year when we go to budget we will know what our hit ratio was and what our closing ratio was. Therefore, we will know how many names to put into next year's campaign.

Once upon a time we could only do that on a mainframe computer but now, with PCs on our desks and notebook computers on the road, we can do it from anywhere.

AN IMPLEMENTATION PRIMER

Tom Peters said, "The only one who really likes change is a wet baby" and that is often what we find when we attempt to implement new technologies and new ways of doing things in our offices.

If a sales software system fails it is usually because sales reps refuse to participate. You will need their buy-in but you will not get it if you fail to implement new technology intelligently and with sensitivity toward the demands you are making on your reps.

How do you do that?

The answer is training. If you are going to involve your sales force you need to introduce them to the software and integrate your nurturing program throughout your organization. If you can do this successfully it will literally change your world. It will change everybody in your organization and it will change your business dramatically.

But first you have to convince your reps that this change is good for them. You have to show them how automating a "stay-in-touch process" will increase their visibility among clients and cultivate new prospects.

In our Nurture Institute training classes we designed fun training programs with real-life drills to demonstrate this.

Have a plan. Systems that work best are those that answer the needs of the internal as well as external reps. The best way to find out those needs is to ask them.

Decide in advance how you will involve sales representatives in designing what they really need. Acknowledge that many top producers are still using Post-it notes and Day-Timers. Do not expect miracles or instant adoption, but know that a few will transition into stardom.

As you work on the design take the opportunity to examine your entire selling process from identifying prospects and integrating the right kind of clients into the system to the challenge of acquiring new skills and adjusting attitudes. Customers and top producers love razzle-dazzle. Plan to include simple multimedia capabilities.

These days any serious marketing plan has to take the Internet into consideration. If you do not already have a selling presence on the Web, you will, even if it is only a billboard and a collection of e-mail addresses for your sales force. Be sure you know how the Web fits into your three-year planning program.

Do not go it alone.

CRM provides solutions with impact at an amazingly low cost. But setting up a CRM program is not as simple as going out and purchasing a program, installing it, and clicking on "run." You and your reps are not technology people. Your expertise is marketing and selling. Your time should be reserved for what you do best.

CRM technology has undergone many incarnations in its evolution and it is safe to assume that there's more to come. Microsoft, SalesLogix, FrontRange Solutions, Touch Points Unlimited, SalesForce.com, and Mastermind Software have produced excellent solutions. Look for the one that best matches your needs.

When you bring in software you either have to buy new or customize what you already have to match your needs and goals. That's a job for IT people - not for the CEO, director of sales and marketing, or anyone whose expertise is marketing and selling. Do not let the task of configuring software distract you from what you do well. Let the techs do what they do well. Just make sure you communicate your needs clearly. Computer people have been known to assume what you need. Remember that these people rarely understand your business. Remember that this is your system and you need to live with it long after the computer folks are gone.

Find an experienced CRM technology partner.

To identify a good one ask if they are certified by a recognized vendor. Find out how long they have been certified. This will give you an idea of how much experience they have with the program. Ask what specific improvements their software will help you achieve in terms of your main business objective.

Find out if other businesses of your size and type have installed, tested, and measured the results. Find out what changes you will have to make in your organization and sales process in order to take total advantage of the software. You will want to know what kind of training your reps will need to become comfortable with the solution and how long the training will take; reps hate to be taken out of the field for extended periods.

You will want to know to what extent the product will have to be modified to integrate with your existing system and get an estimate of the total cost per employee.

Ask for references. Who else is using the software and what is their experience?

Finally, you can outsource.

This is the point where we'll pause, smile and say "...and now a word from our sponsor" because assembling and executing nurture plans for clients is exactly what we do at the Nurture Institute.

If you want to outsource your nurturing campaigns, we're here—list generation, managing your lists, composing letters on your stationary with your signature, sending the appropriate enclosures and e-mail notifications of events, writing call scripts, and assembling the perfect mailings with assured on-time delivery.

It may sound like a daunting task, but monitoring the attitudes, values, visions, demands, and goals of (at least) your "A" clients on a regular basis is something that can easily be accomplished using today's software.

The nurturing system orchestrates a series of highly tailored messages to a select group of your most qualified opportunities. This would have been virtually impossible a decade ago without effective software tools. Today's CRM software has made it possible for companies of any size to become aware of and track not only their individual clients' needs and expectations but also to stay in touch and address their distinct needs and expectations.

Being able to efficiently store and manage a database of valuable client information, cultivate long term relationships, and track a client's lifetime value makes the expense and generic nature of mass marketing messages obsolete. Add nurture to the mix and you have the ability to create personal, long-lasting client relationships.

Nurturing techniques used with today's automated technology offer the tools you need to analyze and solve most marketing or sales issues. With them you can maintain contact with clients while collecting relevant marketing information through questionnaires, surveys, or conversations on a regular basis. This information becomes your source for better serving and retaining clients.

We are living in an era of scientific marketing, of database marketing that gives us the ability to communicate with people on a one-on-one basis in a multitude of ways. Technology has transformed us. We have almost become our own ad agencies, communicating one-on-one with the individuals in that database.

When we begin nurturing we have no idea of the changes that will take place in our lives. They are all centered on communications exchanged between human beings. The people who can ride that change and adapt to technologies that allow us to create authentic relationships will emerge as the leaders in their industry.

Chapter VII–
Managing for Change

"Don't judge each day by the harvest you reap, but by the seeds you plant."

Robert Louis Stevenson

CONTENTS

THE AGE OF RELATIONSHIPS

Solid customer relationships are vitally important to our success in business. We can see that because of the direct impact they have on revenue. But there are many other equally important relationships that benefit from nurturing that might not, at first, be obvious.

Many people tell me, "I have three constituencies to nurture. I have customers. I have prospects and I have staff and suppliers I wish to nurture." It is that third constituency I want to talk about now.

Nurturing is much more than just a marketing strategy. The philosophy stresses continual communications that demonstrate caring and appreciation. By nurturing internally, by tending to our own garden with processes that implement and measure the effects of our interactions with employees just as we do with our customers, we reap harvests that have a tremendous impact on the bottom line.

Often we're so involved in our businesses that we fail to recognize the many contributions that those around us bring to the business. Your employees, like your customers, need to know you understand and appreciate them. Nurturing employees is a matter of human relations and good human relations is good business.

I have a friend in California who owns a regional intermodal trucking company. Trucking is very difficult to differentiate. He decided he wanted to move his business out of a position where his service was viewed as a commodity and into one where it was perceived by customers as a true value-add.

He understood the importance of nurturing in repositioning the company. In addition to the letters he sent to his customers he created a series of letters to go out to his employees. He decided to thank, by name, the 28 of his 480 employees who had perfect attendance the year before.

About a year later his controller told him "you must be doing something right. Last year we had 28 employees with perfect attendance. This year we had 77." He hadn't really thought much about those letters; no one really commented on them. But it occurred to him that maybe the employees were responding to that seemingly insignificant gesture of appreciation. Maybe it was important that they knew he noticed.

Then, another year passed and the controller came in again and said "this year we had 158 with perfect attendance." The simple act of recognizing those whose loyalty made a difference to the firm had a direct impact on the attitudes and morale of his employees and an indirect, but significant, impact on efficiencies in his firm.

True drip irrigation is a systematic process of structuring caring touches that let others know you appreciate them and are there to help them with their pain. This is as true for employees as it is for customers. Nurturing creates a culture of caring and of decency and of permanency. It gives the CEO a methodology for developing a nurturing environment throughout the company.

True nurturing requires the CEO to take a new role. I like to call it the CRO, Chief Relationship Officer.

Why is that the role of the CEO? It is usually the CEO who suffers when nurturing events are left undone. It is the CEO who sees revenues drop when customers defect and employee turnover is high. It is the CEO who has to deal with the impact that those effects have on the bottom line.

PASSION AS DIFFERENTIATOR

In his book, *A Passion for Excellence: The Leadership Difference*, Tom Peters tells us that the hallmark of a truly excellent company is leaders who have a passion for the business and whose passion is shared by their employees.

Passion is a differentiator. No one knows this better than my co-author and business associate, Eric Rabinowitz. Eric's own story demonstrates the power of nurturing, internally and externally, better than any I know.

As I mentioned in an earlier chapter, I had worked with Eric for two years on a nurturing campaign for his company, IHS Helpdesk, back in the mid-1990s.

IHS Helpdesk provides on-site technical support to companies that outsource their high-tech helpdesk staffing needs. Within eight months of launching a nurturing campaign customer requisitions for technical help had risen six-fold. Sales were projected to top $13 million that year but success exposed a new problem. Actual revenue was projected to run closer to $11 million because of the high turnover among helpdesk employees. Turnover was a walloping 300 percent. Even worse, about 30 percent of the new employees recruited each month weren't staying until the month was out. High turnover was not uncommon among high-tech workers back then but it was unacceptable to Eric.

On average IHS Helpdesk employees stayed about 3.5 months. Eric and his partner estimated the company could save $60,000 per year in recruiting fees and administrative costs if they nudged that average up to 3.8 months, $275,000 if they boosted it to seven months, and an unbelievable $2.9 million if they raised it to 18 months. Those numbers didn't even touch lost opportunities due to the number of requisitions that were going unfulfilled.

Eric brought in consultants to tackle the problem realizing it is always a good strategy to tap the expertise of others who have more experience in an area than oneself. The consultants interviewed the group and found that employees at remote job sites often identified more with the client company than with IHS Helpdesk. Many, too, thought of themselves as "temps" and what lured them away was their desire for a "career." Others did not realize the benefits and opportunities of staying at IHS Helpdesk. In short, they needed to know they were loved. They needed nurturing.

Eric launched a nurturing program for all of his employees. He treated new employees to a full day of events at company headquarters in New York City, complete with orientation, educational sessions and, just to make it memorable, a tour of nearby Madison Square Garden. The company began offering their employees training during periods of downtime between assignments and Eric hired an assistant to stay in touch with field reps in a proactive way.

The assistant began calling every employee at every job site at least once a week to say hello, help them with problems, and keep them apprised of employee events like the company picnic. They launched a newsletter called the *Daily Helping* and filled it with technical tips, information about benefits and incentives, kudos on employee accomplishments, inspirational quotes, trivia games, and contests and they faxed it to every employee at their job site each day.

Guess what happened. Within a year the annual rate of resignations fell from 300 to 25 percent. The rate of resignations in the first three months dropped from 30 to 12 ½ percent. And there was a surprise in those numbers. Customer satisfaction went up. Revenues soared from 11 to $15 million and the high retention rate became a differentiator for IHS Helpdesk, itself. It became part of the company's unique selling proposition.

CEO AS VISIONARY

Eric's experience demonstrates the power of working "on" a business rather than always working "in" the business. By stepping outside a daily routine in which he was putting out fires and seeking new recruits he was able to look at the reasons behind those situations and create a strategy to do something about them.

That strategy was "nurturing" which, in our opinion, is the best strategy to use in any area where relationships impact results.

The company that nurtures customers needs to nurture internally as well. Certainly, if we wish to reposition our companies to become more customer-centric we need to communicate our new direction to our staff and allies. And we need to be true to ourselves.

You have heard the adage about practicing what you preach. Our own organizations need to support and reflect the values we communicate to the market.

Wes Snow put that principal to work at Ascendix two years after he launched the company to resell computer technologies. He realized the company's sales performance was a result of collecting low-hanging fruit and that they were competing only for customers who were already ready to buy. He began to focus on strategies that would cultivate long-term relationships in order to generate future sales.

Wes began to identify business strategies and put processes in place to nurture relationships that would deliver over the long term. He surveyed his clients, asking questions such as, "Do you like us?", and got a resounding, "Yes." But when asked if their interaction with Ascendix resulted in business improvements a majority of customers said they were not sure.

That triggered an introspective response in which managers throughout Ascendix asked at every turn, "How can we add more value?"

That is when Wes discovered nurture marketing. He found it to be totally in line with his attempts to transform the business. The whole philosophy immediately resonated with him.

It allowed him to start thinking more as a strategist and a business owner and not just as a person with a great idea. It allowed him to add value layers to the business and take it to the next level.

Wes put nurture marketing to work internally and externally at Ascendix nurturing customers with frequent high-value communications even as he began turning the sales and marketing staffs— everyone who touched the customer—into nurturing experts.

"No one who was involved with our organization back then would recognize who we are today," Wes tells me. He says, "Nurturing allowed us to go to market with a strategy that was almost a complete overhaul of our business."

And what impact has it had on his bottom line?

Today, Ascendix is a leader in enabling technology-based business solutions in the real estate investment and management industry. As a reseller of SalesLogix CRM systems, Ascendix has found itself in the President's Club of top revenue-producing partners for five years running.

BUILDING THE TEAM

When we look at the power of nurturing and what it takes to build a nurturing team we start with the position of the sales manager.

One of the most critical jobs in creating and maintaining a nurturing environment is sales leadership. What other job in the office is more directly responsible for the mission of attracting and keeping customers than that of sales manager? Just as the CEO sets the vision for the company, the sales manager is the one who must implement it.

The key ingredient to success in sales management is not drive. It is heart.

If you are truly going to be successful as a leader, others must be willing to get behind you and move in the direction you are moving. The sales manager must be more than simply a manager—he or she must be a leader. The difference between leadership and management is that management hires and fires but leadership inspires.

The sales manager must create an effective environment where people can produce at their maximum and enjoy it. That requires a sales cultivation process. Just as every business needs a process for handling an order, every business also needs a process for attracting, selecting, and hiring sales people.

Whether you are replacing people on a daily basis, building a team for the first time, or you are simply thinking about what you want your business to become in a year or two, you will ultimately need a process. So what do you do?

If you are the one tasked with team-building, begin by identifying candidates with the skill sets, characteristics, and qualifications that will enhance your nurture team.

DEMONSTRATE VIGOROUSLY

The right training is clearly as important as effective recruiting. Know that the perfect sales person for your organization is not going to magically appear in the doorway.

Once you have matched the attributes and attitudes of your recruits as closely as possible to the skills and behaviors necessary for the job, you can determine the exact training they will require. Today, it is not enough to hire gunslingers. You must teach them how to shoot.

I remember my first day on the job as a sales representative with Smith Corona. The company supplied me with a copying machine, a child's American Flyer wagon, a map with a yellow line around a piece of Louisville, and sent me out. The training program was on the back of the map. The instructions were as follows:

> Once you have the copier working and the wagon wheels oiled, haul the copier to the tallest building in your territory. Go to the top floor and work your way down knocking on doors.

Now comes the training part. It said:

As soon as someone lets you in, demonstrate vigorously.

Then came the motivational part. It said:

When you have sold your first copier you will have a way to support your family.

And at the bottom of the map it said:

We are behind you!

Of course, I add a bit more humor to that story each time I tell it, but I will never forget the experience. That fairly sums up "sales training" in those days. I have met many sales people who started out more or less the same way. Such lack of training is not good enough today.

When training is needed, it should be customized for a person's needs. Customized training is a part of every successful organization. It should not waste a person's time and energy in a classroom.

Internet resources available today make it possible to deliver customized training directly to a person's desktop. The sales manager does not have to be the trainer, but must be the one to identify training that is appropriate and that will have a real impact on knowledge and performance.

THE EFFECTIVE EXECUTIVE

An ancient parable and guide for today:

"Listen! A farmer went out to sow his seed. As he was scattering the seed, some fell along the path,

and the birds came and ate it up. Some fell on rocky places, where it did not have much soil. It sprang up quickly, because the soil was shallow. But when the sun came up, the plants were scorched, and they withered because they had no root. Other seed fell among thorns, which grew up and choked the plants so that they did not bear grain. Still other seed fell on good soil. It came up, grew and produced a crop, multiplying thirty, sixty, or even a hundred times."

As we near the end of this book we would like to finish on the same note on which we began—with the metaphor of the farmer. By now you surely agree that nurturing a garden and bringing it to harvest is the perfect metaphor for building solid customer relationships.

In any business organization, the person who assumes the role of the gardener is the one who cultivates strong relationships. It is the gardener who creates and implements a marketing plan to communicate the right messages to the right people at the right time. The philosophy, methodology, and processes involved in nurturing customer relationships are analogous to adding Miracle-Gro® to your garden—it produces abundant, long-term harvests. Imagine how it will feel when customers consistently come back to you, and also relate their positive experience to others!

Successful CEOs, and sales and marketing managers find time for planting and nurturing. As we said at the outset, nurturing requires patience and persistence. The payoff is always worth the effort.

Here's to abundant harvests!

Appendix I — Prospect Grading Tool

SIMPLE PROSPECT GRADING TABLE

Purpose: To Recognize and Target Viable Prospects

1. On paper, or in a word processing or spreadsheet program, create a table similar to Figure A below:

Criteria	A	B	C	D

Figure A: Blank prospect grading table

2. In the Criteria row, list criteria that identify your very best "A" clients.

   - For example, "fast growth—has more than 1 Billion in Revenue," or "particularly willing to invest in new technology", or any other description you have identified as typical of your very best clients.

3. In this version of the table, the A, B, C, and D columns represent your A, B, C, and D clients. For each client type, assign a descriptor that corresponds with each criterion.

   For example, if the size of a client's sales team is one of your criteria, assign each client type a potential sales force size. Your "A" clients might have a sales force size of 20-50; your "B" clients might have a force of 10-20, etc.

   Figure B, below shows a completed example. Note that this example only lists six criteria, but your table can have as many rows as necessary.

Criteria	A	B	C	D
Size of sales team	20-50	15-20	10-15	>9
Invest in new tech	Very high	High	Moderate	Low
Invoice payment schedule	On invoice	30 days	60 days	90+ days
Inside champion	FT	PT	Consultant	None
Uses consultants	Always	Frequently	Occasionally	Never
Enlightened management	Highly	Willing	Moderately	Low

Figure B: Table with grading criteria for each client type

4. For each prospect you want to evaluate, make a new table with the prospect's name at the top. The table grid should contain the same list of criteria used in the previous table. Leave the A, B, C, and D columns blank for now, and add a Total row at the bottom of the table.

5. Use this new table to grade each prospect against the listed criteria.

   • The point value for each A, B, C, or D grade is as follows: A=4, B=3, C=2, and D=1.

- You can give a prospect an A+ by assigning a 4.5 or 5 point value. You can give a prospect a B-/C+ by assigning a 2.5 point value.

6. In the Total column, enter the total of the prospect's grades, then calculate their grade point average.

   - A completed example is shown below. Note that this example only lists six criteria – your table can have as many as you need.

Criteria	A	B	C	D	Subtotal
Size of sales team		3			3
Invest in new tech		3			3
Invoice payment schedule		3			3
Inside champion	4				4
Uses consultants	4				4
Enlightened management	4				4
				TOTAL	21

Figure C: Graded prospect with a GPA of 3.5

7. Divide the number in the Total cell by the number of criteria to determine the prospect's GPA (grade point average).

In Figure C, the prospect's GPA is 3.5 (21/6), so this prospect could potentially be either an "A" or a "B" client and is well worth your Nurturing efforts.

Appendix I – Prospect Grading Tool

Appendix II—Sample Drip Irrigation Plan

GENERIC PROSPECTING – B TO B EXECUTIVE

Purpose: Ensure Top of Mind Positioning

Step	Days	Activity	Description	Enclosure
Step 1 A&B	0	Letter	Personal Introduction	Brochure
STEP 2	15	Gift/ Offer	Business @ the Speed of Thought	Book Summary
STEP 3	40	Letter	Positioning	
STEP 4	15	Gift	Specific "Industry Pain"	Article Shredded Money
STEP 5	15	Invite	Invitation to briefing	Invitation
STEP 6	5	Phone Script	Follow-up	"Is You Is'
STEP 7	20	Offer	Briefing Highlights	Offer
STEP 8	7	Phone Script	After Event Follow-up	
STEP 9	30	Letter	Article of Interest	Article
STEP 10	30	Letter	Trans- formation	Article
STEP 11	30	Offer	Industry (Company)	White Paper on Chief Pain
STEP 12	Seasonal		Holiday Greeting	Thanksgiving

> **Step 1A Sample Letter:** *The Personal Introduction. When you know who makes the decision and wish to make direct contact, try this approach. Getting the attention of the reader, especially a business executive, requires specific, to the point communiqués that are soft but direct. The example below gives you a model you can refine for your letter of introduction.*

Mr. John Daniels
5454 Fourth Ave.
Seattle, WA 98006

Dear John,

The real world demands clear-cut, tangible results that are often obtained only with hands-on involvement. And you and I both know that is possible only when you have solutions with built-in simplicity —solutions that are easy to understand and use.

That is the reason I am writing to you today. My name is Jim Miller *(title)* of   (<u>*company*</u>). While you and I have never met or had any prior business interaction, I wanted to introduce myself and our company, and let you know that we provide very valuable solutions to problems such as   (<u>*specific*</u>)   and   (<u>*specific*</u>).

May I stay in touch with you from time to time to keep you abreast of opportunities and strategies we provide for efficiently controlling problems such as *(problem)* ?

At (_company_), you will find knowledgeable, professional people who think the way you do and who can help you maintain the performance you want with consistent results.

Thank you for your time!

Sincerely,

Jim Miller
President

Enc. Brochure

> **Step 1B Sample Letter:** *You've hit gold. Now you need to mine it. You've discovered a solution for a problem of a substantial company. If successful, you'll earn a lifetime of gratitude as well as money. All you need to do is access the right person at the right executive level. This letter should take a stronger approach than the one in Step 1A to engage in a serious, one-to-one conversation.*

Mr. John Daniels
5454 Fourth Ave.
Seattle, WA 98006

Dear John,

Although I have not had any interaction with you or your company, I am writing to you because I am searching for the most appropriate key executive in *(company)* to invite to our "(Presentation Title)" — an overview of solutions we provide to solve   (*specific problem*).

Our business is helping people in your industry utilize (your product) to leverage the investment they have made in (sales force or reseller channel, etc). The net benefits we deliver are   (*benefit one*),   (*benefit two*) and (*benefit three*). Some of the customers we have helped are   (*customer*),   (*customer*), and (*customer*).

We are locally owned, globally focused, and grounded in (specific) solutions and we are proud of our position as a premier   (*specific*)   firm in the   (*area*).

In an effort to be a good steward of your time, we've done some preliminary background research on your company and understand from visiting your website that your near-term goals are to (*goal*), (*goal*), and (*goal*).

If you will grant me an appointment, I will present:

- Unique opportunities to (*benefit one*).
- Two specific steps to leverage (*benefit two*).
- Three simple ways to (*benefit three*).

I do not need to speak with you directly, but will contact your administrative assistant in the next two to four days to set up the meeting date and time should you be interested.

Thank you for your time and I hope to meet you soon,

Sincerely,

Jim Miller
President

Enc. Brochure

Step 2 Sample Letter: *No gift is more appreciated in business relationships than a book, either hard-copy or condensed version. Nearly every business pain has been described in a book. Send one that's appropriate to your prospect's pain with a variation on this letter in which we offered Bill Gates's Business @ the Speed of Thought. View and Order Executive Book Summaries at www.summary.com*

Mr. John Daniels
5454 Fourth Ave.
Seattle, WA 98006

> **"I have a simple but strong belief. The most meaningful way to differentiate your company from your competition, the best way to put distance between you and the crowd, is to do an outstanding job with information. How you gather, manage and use information will determine whether you win or lose."** — *Bill Gates*

Dear John,

With the words quoted above, a man who is unquestionably one of this century's most visionary leaders opened his latest book, *Business @ the Speed of Thought*.

Creating unique and memorable customer experiences often demands flexible, custom solutions. You are the only one who knows exactly which information system will mean the difference between mediocre performance and dynamic growth and success for your business. The enclosed summary might spark your interest in knowing how other great thinkers implement business solutions for their companies.

If you would like a personal copy of the full edition, check the box below and fax this letter back to me. We will send the book to you with our best wishes.

Sincerely,

Jim Miller
President

Enc. *Business @ the Speed of Thought* Book Summary

☐ Yes, I'd like a personal copy of *Business @ the Speed of Thought*

Step 3 Positioning Sample Letter: *The chief reason people fail to respond to sales letters is that most are impersonal and bland. Help the reader to get your message and understand your positioning by seeing it through the eyes of another.*

Mr. John Daniels
5454 Fourth Ave.
Seattle, WA 98006

Dear John,

I got a call from an old friend the other day with an interesting question. He asked me what made us different from the other   (*industry*)   firms. It was surprisingly easy for me to answer.

(*Tell your own story here*)

"From the first day we opened, we told our people and the world that our mission is to help clients achieve success. Simply put, it means that we do whatever it takes to make our customers successful. Today, you measure success by what a   (*solution provider*)   can bring to the table beyond   (*Example....software — shorter sales cycles, quicker resolution of service issues, and more customer value delivered over time and at each stage.*)

(*Enumerate your value and values here*)

 "We believe the true value of your organization's data lies in your ability to   (*Benefit example: make information work throughout your enterprise.*)   And that means creating and maintaining systems and business methods that can maximize data quickly and efficiently in order to support a workforce and serve customers well. That's the bottom line — our clients want solutions, not just products. They want solutions to make sure:

(*Specific ways your clients benefit*)

- You can stay closely connected to your customers
- That you know what they want and the way they want it
- That you have what they want to buy when they want to buy it
- That your employees can meet their needs in real time
  (*Your ultimate benefit*)

"We make that success possible with the most functionally complete closed-loop sales, marketing, and customer service solutions available. Through solid alliances with world-class partners, we provide unrivaled business systems like (Great Plains, Microsoft, and Siebel Systems) solutions for both the back and front office. We help clients blend the right hardware and intelligent software solutions with our systematic and responsive customer service and support infrastructure."

"But well beyond software and technology, at (*company*),   our clients really do come first and they always will. To make that happen, we start with the quality of people we select — a basic requirement is they must naturally like serving customers. If there is a technical problem, we immediately deploy the right resources necessary to resolve it — whenever and wherever required."

So that's what I told him. It was good to say it out loud to that old friend, because frankly that is who we are.

And I believe that is part of the reason   (*company*) has twice been named   (*award*).

I believe when you review the enclosed corporate information, you will see for yourself that we are truly large enough to intelligently solve and small enough to enthusiastically serve.

Sincerely,

Jim Miller
President

> **Step 4 Specific "Industry Pain" Sample Letter:**
> Articles can say volumes about your focus, your level of thinking and how you demonstrate what you know about prospects and their industries. By spending an hour or less on Google, you'll find volumes of relevant articles, white papers and books that can help ease clients' pain. You'll want to print the articles and include them as enclosures in letters, explaining your reason for the selection. It is a great way to make solid contacts of genuine value. The following letter references an article we found at www.hospitalconnect.com. To make a point about value, we included shredded money purchased from www.educationalcoin.com where you can order defunct currencies.

Mr. John Daniels
5454 Fourth Ave.
Seattle, WA 98006

"Ignoring underutilized assets is a lot like shredding money."

— *Malcolm Forbes*

Dear John,

Ever read a definition of value? One dictionary says it is, "The amount of resources one is willing to invest."

During periods of rapidly shifting economies, we need a clear appreciation of our values and of the ways we measure value.

Healthcare facilities across the country face daunting issues from skilled worker shortages to funding challenges and the frightening specter of an aging population – all of which tends to shred cash.

In a recent article "Health Facilities Management Executive Dialog Service," a number of hurdles facing the industry were explored. I thought you might find some of the panel's insights as helpful as I did.

Sincerely,

Jim Miller
President

Enc: Shredded Money, Article

> **Step 5 Sample Letter:** *A personal invitation to a well-conceived knowledge-based webinar often gets interested prospects to raise their hands and be recognized.*

Mr. John Daniels
5454 Fourth Ave.
Seattle, WA 98006

"Occasionally sharpen your saw."

Steven Covey

Dear John,

From time to time, partners in our firm invite   *(title of invitee)*   and CEO's for an evening of shirtsleeve conversations and specific   *(subject)*   presentations. It is often an excellent opportunity to review changes and other pressing challenges of dealing with *(challenge)*   and *(challenge)*.   Respected members of allied professions often join us, making these evening briefings stimulating, unique, and invaluable.

(*Title of Briefing*)

As another method of staying in touch, I would like to invite you to join us for our upcoming "(*Title of Briefing*)." I am enclosing a more detailed invitation for your review and ask that you fax or phone names of individuals who might enjoy joining us for this special evening.

The evening promises to be a fast paced and fascinating look at   (*subject*). We'd love to have you join us.

Sincerely,

Jim Miller
President

Enc. Invitation

> **Step 6 Sample Script:** *Most sales are lost because of failure to follow up. Even if that were only half true, think of the opportunities you could generate by calling a prospect personally to confirm the invitation. This phone script references the old song "Is You Is Or Is You Ain't My Baby?" to engage the prospect and help you evaluate the prospect's interest, power, pain, budget, process, and potential. It also allows removal of those who are clearly inappropriate, not qualified, or not interested.*

May I speak with (_prospect_)?

Hello, I am (_name_) from (_company_).

Is this a good time for us to talk or should I call you later?

YES: Continue...

NO: Find a good time and call at that time.

I wrote you recently inviting you to our "(_Briefing Title_)" briefing and I called to see if you had time to review the invitation and if you plan on attending.

YES: Should I go ahead and register you?

NO: Is there someone else more appropriate for this type of briefing?

Do you routinely use (_services like ours_)?

YES:

NO: Is there someone in your firm who has that responsibility?

Do you believe you might have a reason in the future for knowing a firm such as (_company_) ?

May we continue to send you our newsletters, etc?

Prefer   Print____   Email____

address_____

What resources do you currently use for   (*our services*)?

Get info.

Would it be appropriate for us to meet with you to review your challenges in more detail? We'll personally answer any questions you might have.

What time is good for you next week?

DATE: _____   TIME: _____

_____

NO: Can we stay in touch and send you information from time to time?

Verify name, title, address

Thanks for speaking with me.

> **Step 7 Sample Letter:** *Those who intended to attend your event but, for whatever reason did not attend, they are often neglected. They are, however, well worth further exploration because they have demonstrated interest. Follow up with a short briefing on the highlights of the event. Since they have acknowledged at least some interest, why not encourage further conversations, questions or purchase? Don't miss this opportunity to make another personal touch.*

Mr. John Daniels
5454 Fourth Ave.
Seattle, WA 98006

Dear John,

A couple of very exciting things happened the other night at our "(*Briefing Title*)" briefing.

1. A number of very innovative and far-reaching strategies were highlighted and discussed.

2. We had a tape running and were able to capture the best ideas and condense this briefing into a short, tight, drive-time-friendly audiocassette/CD.

I promised those attending that I would continue to explore new ideas and proven tactics and to keep all advised. If you would like more detailed information or an audiocassette/CD of the evening, check the box below and fax it back to us. We'll do the rest.

Sincerely,

Jim Miller
President

Please Fax this Information Card to 732 636-8733

Attention: Jim Cecil

☐ Please send me more information on (*product/services*)   strategies.

☐ Please send me the audiocassette/CD.

☐ Please notify me of future briefings.

> **Step 8 Sample Phone Script:** *The best time to talk to a prospect is within days of the event, whether they attended or registered but failed to attend. Either way, you know that the people you are calling have expressed an interest in your company or your solution. They deserve a personal follow-up. This call is not an attempt to sell; rather, it is an opportunity to determine exactly where things stand. It lets you gather information that will prescribe your next step.*

Version 1 - <u>Live phone contact</u>

- Introduce self
- Reason for call
- As your personal (*account manager*) at (*company*), I know how busy your life is and I wanted just a couple of minutes to say hello personally and to (*get an update from you about your project*.)
- We've been writing to you and I wanted to ask if the materials we send seem relevant and if it is acceptable that I continue to stay in touch that way.
- At our last executive briefing, we taped the presentation and would be glad to provide a CD or cassette if you are interested, naturally with our compliments.
- I wanted to suggest we might meet for lunch and go over your ideas and plans. In your opinion, do you feel a face-to-face meeting would be helpful? (Use your sensitivity to determine the appropriateness of this approach.)
- (If No Lunch) Is there anything we might do that would be of value to you at this point?
- Cordial closing comments and articulate appropriate next steps.

Version 2 - <u>Voice Mail Edition</u>

Hi, this is (*name*) at (*company*). Sorry I missed you but voice mail will do just fine. I merely called to get a project update to make sure we stay on track with you.

- We've been writing to you and I wanted to ask if the materials we've been sending seem relevant and if it is acceptable that I continue to stay in touch this way.
- I also wanted to find out (if you don't already know) if you have selected all the firms to (*manage your project*) and if there is anything we might do that would be of value to you at this point?
- At our last executive briefing, we taped the presentation and would be glad to provide a CD or cassette if you are interested, naturally with our compliments.
- Please let me know if you would like to meet and go over any plans you have thus far for your project.

Meanwhile, thanks for your interest in (*company*) and I look forward to talking with you.

> **Step 9 Sample Letter:** *People tend to like others who share a similar point of view. Sales pros have long scoured publications that their best prospects and customers read and once in a while an article comes along that really hits a big issue between the eyes. Finding and storing such articles of interests make it easy to use the content later to make an impact.*

Mr. John Daniels
5454 Fourth Ave.
Seattle, WA 98006

Dear John,

You can imagine that helping firms keep up with their *(business problems you solve)* day in and day out makes us pay very close attention to the entire issue of *(key issue of the day)*. I find myself reading more *(your specific)* industry specific periodicals now than at any time before.

Once in a while an article comes along that is poignant as well as timely. I think that *(author's name)*'s recent commentary on *(topic)* provided a wonderful overview of the philosophies and technologies driving the *(your specific)* industry.

I'm enclosing a copy in case you missed it. Hope it proves interesting. If there are questions or if we can assist you any way, please know I'm here to help.

Sincerely,

Jim Miller
President

Enc. Article of interest to your client

> ***Step 10 Sample Letter:*** *Every continuous contact campaign should include an occasional letter that simply states, "I thought of you as a person as well as a prospective customer." The following sample letter, along with the article on the impact of change, has always earned warm responses. It seems to fit into so many situations and makes the reader feel as if it must have been selected personally for them.*

Mr. John Daniels
5454 Fourth Ave.
Seattle, WA 98006

Dear John,

I read a fascinating article the other day about reactions people have when dealing with change. I feel my entire personal and professional life is driven by the speed of information and the technology surrounding it. While computers allow all of us to manage information and communications better, the speed of that learning curve is moving most of us into *overload* at an ever-accelerating rate.

In reading the article on the *"Fear of Transformation,"* it dawned on me how in the era of techno-change, the transition zone is becoming a place each of us visits almost constantly. I hope you find it as interesting as I did.

Sincerely,

Jim Miller
President

Enc. Transformation Article

FEAR OF TRANSFORMATION

Sometimes I feel that my life is a series of trapeze swings. I'm either hanging on to a trapeze bar swinging along, or for a few moments, I'm hurtling across space in between bars.

Most of the time I'm hanging on for dear life to my trapeze bar of the moment. It carries me along at a certain steady rate of swing and I have the feeling that I'm in control of my life. I know most of the right questions and even some of the right answers. But once in awhile as I'm merrily swinging along, I look ahead of me into the distance and I see another bar swinging towards me. It is empty and I know, in that place in me that *knows*, that this new trapeze bar has *my* name on it. It is my next step, my growth, my aliveness coming to get me. In my heart-of-hearts I know that for me to grow, I must release my grip on the present, well-known bar to move to the new one.

Each time it happens, I hope and pray that I won't have to grab the new trapeze bar. But in my *knowing* place I realize that I must totally release my grasp on my old bar and for some time I must hurtle across space before I can grab onto the new bar. Each time I am filled with terror. It doesn't matter that in all my previous hurtles across the void of unknowing, I have always made it. Each time I am afraid I will miss—that I will be crushed on unseen rocks in the bottomless chasm between the bars. But I do it anyway. Perhaps this is the essence of what the mystics call the faith experience. No guarantees, no net, no insurance policy, but you do it anyway because somehow, to keep hanging onto that old bar is no longer an alternative. And so for an eternity that can last a microsecond or a thousand lifetimes, I soar across the dark void of "the past is gone, the future is not yet here." It is called transition. I have come to believe that it is the only place that real change occurs.

I have noticed that in our culture this transition zone is looked upon as a nothing—a no-place between places. Surely the old trapeze bar was real and that new one coming towards me, I hope that's real, too. But the void in between? That's just a scary, confusing, disorienting "nowhere" that must be gotten through as fast and as unconsciously as possible. What a waste! I have a sneaking suspicion that the transition zone is the only real thing, and that the bars are *illusions* we dream up to avoid the void where the real change, the real growth, occurs for us. Whether or not my hunch is true, it remains that the transition zones in our lives are incredibly rich places. They should be honored—even savored. Even with all the pain and fear and feelings of being out-of-control that can accompany transitions, they are still the most alive, most growth filled, most passionate, most expansive moments in our lives.

And so, transformation of fear may have nothing to do with making fear go away, but rather with giving ourselves permission to "hang out" in the transition between trapeze bars. Transforming our need to grab that *new* bar... any bar... is allowing ourselves to dwell in the only place where change really happens. It can be terrifying. It can also be enlightening, in the true sense of the word. Hurtling through the void—we just may learn how to fly.

by Danaan Parry

> **Step 11 Sample Letter:** *Some buying cycles are prolonged. While that can be frustrating, prolonged cycles do provide excellent opportunities to send intelligent touches that add value, trust, and confidence to your customer relationships. Use prolonged cycles to your advantage by researching white papers and industry briefings that are relevant to the problems and needs of your customers and prospects.*

Mr. John Daniels
5454 Fourth Ave.
Seattle, WA 98006

Dear John,

As an architect of management thinking, Rosabeth Moss Kanter has become a legend by helping businesses navigate change. In her usual 'to the point' style, she defines the radical changes taking place in the very nature of managerial work and describes the five forms change is taking.

1. There are many more channels for instigating action and exerting influence.

2. These channels are more likely to function horizontally, through peers, than vertically, through the chain of command.

3. There are fewer differences between managers and the people they manage especially in terms of information, control over assignments, and access to external relationships.

4. External relationships have become more important sources of internal power and influence.

5. Career development is less structured, with fewer assured routes to promotion but more opportunities for innovation and entrepreneurial success.

Because of her deep insight into the role of human resource development, we pay close attention to her writing. In her acclaimed white paper entitled "The New Managerial Work," she emphasizes that managers must master change in two critical areas — power and motivation — in order to manage effectively in the new organization.

In ordering a number of reprints of this work for our staff, I realized that some of our clients and friends might like a copy of this white paper as well. So if you'd like to have a copy, simply check the box below, fax it back to us and we'll do the rest.

Sincerely,

Jim Miller
President

☐ Yes, please send the white paper.

> **Step 12 Sample Letter:** *While greetings are expected during the holidays, a personally signed greeting makes a lasting impression. They not only thank your reader for allowing you to maintain contact, they also reveal a deeper side to your values*

Mr. John Daniels
5454 Fourth Ave.
Seattle, WA 98006

Dear John,

In a world of abundance and success, Thanksgiving is an especially appropriate time for all of us to think of others. In appreciation for and in honor of our business relationships, I wanted to write and let you know that rather than holiday and seasonal cards this year we are making a corresponding donation to an organization that does wonderful work.

Futures for Children, headquartered in Albuquerque, New Mexico, was chosen for this annual contribution because of the outstanding work they are doing. Their mission is to help end the poverty and social dependence of Native American Indian and aboriginal children worldwide through one-to-one educational contacts and strategies. In reservation schools, children gain hope and self-esteem with access to the internet and regular contact with caring mentors. I feel that our support will make a difference where it counts the most.

From all of us at   (*company*).

Sincerely,

Jim Miller
President

Enc. Charity Brochure

(Use Charity of Your Choice)

Recommended Reading

Ralph Bruksos , *Turning Change into a Payday*. Training Consultants, July 2005 . Relatively few men are called to become doctors or healers but a rare few manage to accomplish both through the steady application of their courage, perseverance, talents, skills, or dedication to the success of others.

Don Peppers and Dr. Martha Rogers, *Enterprise One to One*. Doubleday-Currency Book, 1999. Don Peppers and Dr. Martha Rogers, authors of the international best seller *The One to One Future*, go beyond that now classic work on how to sell more products to fewer customers. For the last several years, they have been teaching companies how to stay at the head of the pack by harnessing technology to achieve killer competitive advantages in customer loyalty.

Seth Godin, *Permission Marketing*. Simon & Shuster, May, 1999. Remember "Mother, May I?" from childhood? It is back and it is deadly serious this time. Permission Marketing evangelist and Internet Marketing Pioneer, Seth Godin, says he wants to change the way almost everything is marketed today. The key question is: will you give him permission to show you the immediate future of true customer relationship management? The man

'Business Week' calls the 'ultimate entrepreneur for the information age,' teaches in-touch and the Nurture message in the age of the digital nervous system better than anyone yet.

Bill Gates, *Business @ The Speed of Thought: Using a Digital Nervous System*. Warner Books, March, 1999. In clear, non-technical language, *Business @ The Speed of Thought* shows you how a digital nervous system can unite all the systems and processes under one common infrastructure, releasing rivers of information and allowing your company to make a quantum leaps in efficiency, growth and profits.

Berndt H. Schmitt, *Experiential Marketing: How to Get Customers to Sense, Feel, Think, Act, and Relate to Your Company and Brands*. Free Press, 1999. Experiential Marketing, a new form of corporate persuasion that strives to elicit a powerful sensory or thoughtful customer response, is rapidly replacing the boring features-and-benefits approach.

Bill Bachrach, *Values-Based Selling: The Art of Building High-Trust Client Relationships*. Bachrach & Associates, 1996. Values-Based Selling is one of the really great books on becoming a trusted financial advisor to affluent people. If you are a financial professional and have not read this book, you are missing out! The author emphasizes the importance of trust and tells how understanding a person's values system can make a world of difference. One could almost say that these ideas originated from Dr. Stephen Covey's *The 7 Habits of*

Highly Effective People. The main difference is that *Values-Based Selling* is specifically for financial advisors.

Tom Sant, The Giants of Sales: What Dale Carnegie, John Patterson, Elmer Wheeler, and Joe Girard Can Teach You About Real Sales Success. Amacom Books, 2006. *The Giants of Sales* introduces readers to the techniques developed by four legendary sales giants and offers concrete examples of how they still work in the 21st century. Part history and part how-to, Sant gives readers practical, real-world techniques based on the time-tested wisdom of true sales masters.

Tom Sant, *Persuasive Business Proposals: Writing to Win Customers, Clients, and Contracts*. Amacom Books, 2003. *Persuasive Business Proposals* cuts to the quick, providing actionable advice on how to respond efficiently and effectively to an RFP. It presents an excellent structure for writing any proposal from start to finish.

Geoffrey Moore, *Crossing the Chasm*. Harper Business, 2002. Here's a book for venture capitalists, high-tech product managers, and technology marketers. Geoffrey Moore's classic on high-tech marketing charts the chasm theory of technology sales. Innovation sells well to tech-savvy "early adopters" but hits a lull when marketers try to "cross the chasm" into the mass market. How do you remedy this? Through careful targeting, Moore says.

Robert B. Cialdini, Ph.D, *Influence: The Psychology of Persuasion*. **Collins, 1998.** If you have ever attempted to sell a product, to persuade a client, to influence another's decision; if you have ever entered a department store or thought about buying life insurance or wondered whether to vote for a presidential candidate - in short, all of us, persuaders and persuaded a dozen times a day—you will be enlightened and delighted by what can be learned from this indispensable book.

Al Reis & Jack Trout, *Bottom-Up Marketing*. **McGraw-Hill Interamericana, 1995.** This book takes you through the process of building a marketing strategy by starting at the bottom and looking for a tactic to exploit. In this pioneering book, Al Reis and Jack Trout explain how marketing should be practiced.

Al Reis & Jack Trout, *Positioning: The Battle For Your Mind*. **McGraw-Hill, 2000.** In the latest edition of this marketing classic, advertising gurus Al Ries and Jack Trout tell how to use ad agency techniques to position yourself as an industry leader and your competition as followers.

Robert J. Richardson, *The Charisma Factor*. **Prentice Hall 1993.** How to develop two vital communication skills, entertainment, a technique that allows charismatic leaders to bond with others quickly and gracefully, and emotional management, a set of techniques used to spark any emotional state of mind in those around you.

Michael E. Gerber, *The E Myth Revisited: Why Most Small Businesses Don't Work and What to Do About It. Collins*, 1995. Michael Gerber dispels the myths surrounding starting your own business and shows how commonplace assumptions can get in the way of running a business. Next, he walks you through the steps in the life of a business–from entrepreneurial infancy, through adolescent growing pains, to the mature entrepreneurial perspective, the guiding light of all businesses that succeed–and shows how to apply the lessons of franchising to any business, whether or not it is a franchise.

Jack Burke, *Creating Customer Connections: How to Make Customer Service a Profit Center for Your Company* (Taking Control Series). Merritt Publishing, 1998. Excellent customer service generates repeat business and strong profit margins. This book breaks down the various facets of customer service and explains how the smart business person can master them all. As author Jack Burke writes, "Success in business requires an integrated marketing and communication approach that will result in the cultivation of a nexus between a company and its customers."

Recommended Reading

About the Authors

Jim Cecil

Jim Cecil is Founder and President of the **James P. Cecil Company, Inc.**, in Bellevue, Washington, and Director of Education for The Nurture Institute in Woodbridge, New Jersey. He is an acknowledged leader in the field of one-to-one marketing and client relationship strategies.

In 1986, Cecil launched his core company, **Nurture Marketing**, to help clients integrate new technologies with emerging sales and marketing software, and to help sales organizations cultivate client relationships.

Jim is the author of *A Cure for the Common Cold Call— 101 Best Nurture Tips,* and co-author of *Nurturing Customer Relationships.*

Cecil is a frequent columnist on nurturing for *Rough Notes Magazine, Business Technology Association Magazine*, and the *Microsoft Insider Magazine.* Cecil's **Nurture Newsletter** is distributed world-wide.

CONTACT INFORMATION

Email:	**jim@nurturemarketing.com**
Telephone:	425-641-3333
Website:	www.nurturemarketing.com
Address:	15600 NE 8th Street, Suite B1
	Bellevue, WA 98008-39581

Eric Rabinowitz

As Co-Founder of **The Nurture Institute** and Chief Executive Officer of **DEMA Education**, Eric Rabinowitz leads all course development for The Institute. DEMA Education develops targeted training programs that help companies in emerging markets increase their strategic value to clients and add new revenue sources through training.

A successful entrepreneur, Rabinowitz helped build **Leveraged Technology Inc.**, a consulting firm in which he served as marketing vice-president and vice-president of sales.

In 1989, Rabinowitz tapped the technical support help desk marketplace and launched the highly successful **IHS Support Solutions**, a consulting, staffing, and training practice.

CONTACT INFORMATION

Email: **erabinowitz@dema-edu.com**
Telephone: 732-636-1001
Website: www.nurtureinstitute.com
Address: 321 Main Street
               Woodbridge, NJ 07095

Carol Ellison

Carol Ellison is principal partner of **Ellison Associates**, specialists in high-tech communications including industry whitepapers, targeted marketing communications, and "stories that sell."

Ellison's reports have appeared in *PC/Magazine*, *CRM magazine*, *VARBusiness*, *HomePC*, *Small Business Computing*, *The Washington Post*, and the *Christian Science Monitor*. She has appeared as an industry expert on numerous television shows, including *Oprah* and *CNN*.

For more about Ellison Associates, please visit **www.cellison.com.**

Karin Rex

Karin Rex is a nationally known writer as well as founder and owner of **ComputerEase**, a provider of customized technology and sales training.

Rex is a pioneer in online learning. She has designed custom learning experiences for e-learning industry leaders such as Element K, SmartPlanet, and Powered, Inc.

For more about Karin Rex, please visit **www.karinrex.com**

The Nurture Institute

The Nurture Institute™, a **DEMA Education Company,** provides **Nurture Selling Process**® classroom training as well as **Nurture Marketing™** fulfillment under the senior management team of Jim Cecil, Eric Rabinowitz and Jeff Leska, COO for DEMA Education.

Nurture Selling Process® Training

The Nurture Institute™ offers a comprehensive training program in the **Nurture Selling Process**® developed by Jim Cecil. The Institute helps organizations cultivate and maintain top-of-mind presence with clients and prospects by creating and effectively managing ongoing, personalized letter, and phone contact campaigns. Clients benefit from shorter selling cycles, reduced turnover, and increases in both sales productivity and client satisfaction.

For additional information on Nurture Institute's training, including a list of upcoming courses, visit **www.nurtureinstitute.com.**

Nurture Marketing™ Fulfillment Services

The Nurture Institute™ creates, implements, and manages customized client touch campaigns and action plans, all of which are based on Jim Cecil's Nurture Marketing methodology.

For additional information on Nurture Institute's fulfillment services, please call
732-636-1001 x27.

About the Authors